The Crucified Is My Love

The Crucified Is My Love

Morning and Evening Devotions
for the Holy Season of Lent

JOHANN ERNST VON HOLST

Translated by Kathleen Hasenberg
Edited by Emmy Barth Maendel

PLOUGH PUBLISHING HOUSE

Published by Plough Publishing House
Walden, New York
Robertsbridge, England
Elsmore, Australia
www.plough.com

Plough produces books, a quarterly magazine, and Plough.com to encourage people and help them put their faith into action. We believe Jesus can transform the world and that his teachings and example apply to all aspects of life. At the same time, we seek common ground with all people regardless of their creed.

Plough is the publishing house of the Bruderhof, an international Christian community. The Bruderhof is a fellowship of families and singles practicing radical discipleship in the spirit of the first church in Jerusalem (Acts 2 and 4). Members devote their entire lives to serving God, one another, and their neighbors, renouncing private property and sharing everything. To learn more about the Bruderhof's faith, history, and daily life, see Bruderhof.com. (Views expressed by Plough authors are their own and do not necessarily reflect the position of the Bruderhof.)

Translated from *Der am Kreuz ist meine Liebe: Morgen– und Abendandachten für alle Tage der heiligen Passionszeit* by J. E. v. Holst (Riga, Verlag von R. Rymmel, 1895). Illustrations by Rudolf Koch, from *Das Leben Jesu,* Bärenreiter-Verlag: Kassel, 1934. Front cover: Caspar David Friedrich, *Cross in the Mountains,* oil on canvas, Galerie Neue Meister, Dresden, Germany. © Staatliche Kunstsammlungen Dresden / Bridgeman Images. Scripture is from *The Holy Bible, English Standard Version.* Copyright © 2001 by Crossway Bibles, a publishing ministry of Good News Publishers.

A catalog record for this book is available from the British Library.
Library of Congress Cataloging-in-Publication Data
Names: Von Holst, Johann Ernst, 1828-1898, author.
Title: The crucified is my love : morning and evening devotions for the holy season of Lent / Johann Ernst von Holst.
Other titles: Der Am Kreuz ist meine Liebe. English
Description: Walden : Plough Publishing House, 2017. | Hymns and prayers contained in original German have been omitted.
Identifiers: LCCN 2017024459 (print) | LCCN 2017038035 (ebook) | ISBN 9780874861020 (epub) | ISBN 9780874861198 (mobi) | ISBN 9780874861235 (pdf) | ISBN 9780874860429 (pbk.)
Subjects: LCSH: Lent--Meditations.
Classification: LCC BV85 (ebook) | LCC BV85 .V6613 2017 (print) | DDC 242/.34--dc23
LC record available at https://lccn.loc.gov/2017024459

Contents

Second Week of Lent

Third Week of Lent

Fourth Week of Lent

Fifth Week of Lent

Sixth Week of Lent

Preface

JOHANN ERNST VON HOLST (1828–1898) was a
Lutheran pastor in the Baltic country of Latvia. In
the 1800s Latvia had a strong German population
that dated to the thirteenth century. These Germans
were for the most part upright, community-minded
citizens, deeply grounded in their Lutheran faith. Riga,
the capital, was part of the Hanseatic League; its citizens were merchants. (Around 1890, Russia took over
Latvia, forcing the Germans to emigrate to Germany
or to accept "Russification" of their schools and public
institutions.)

Von Holst served as pastor in Wenden (today Cesis).
He was remembered for his lively narrations of Bible
stories and detailed descriptions, particularly in his
children's sermons and confirmation classes. In 1877 he
became senior pastor in the St. James Church in Riga.
He was president of the board of Riga's Magdalene
Asylum – a home that gave women who had nowhere

else to go work and accommodation.[1] He retired as pastor at Pentecost 1890 and died July 26, 1898.

Von Holst published a history and character sketch of the prophet Elijah in 1893, *Der Prophet Elias: Ein alttestamentliches Geschichts- und Charakterbild.* A review of a collection of his sermons in 1876 described them as "fresh and spirit-filled," "a real treasure, indisputably among the best homiletic literature of the Lutheran church." "The sermons embrace all aspects of our inner life and vary in their tone. Sometimes it is the inviting love of the Savior, sometimes the dead seriousness of God's prophets that moves the heart. The biblical interpretation is spiritual, the language noble and simple."[2]

The Lenten devotions in this book were published in 1895, and the author gave a copy of the book to Elise Otto, a member of his congregation at New Year's 1896 (my great-great-grandmother and the grandmother of Bruderhof founders Emmy Arnold and Else von Hollander). It has been passed down and cherished by the family, pulled out and read every Lent. Around 1980 Kathleen Hasenberg, a family friend, translated it into English.

---

1 see *Rigasche Stadtblätter* 1895.
2 *Rigasche Zeitung,* September 23, 1876.

In the original German, each devotion begins with a hymn, followed by the scripture text, the interpretation, a prayer, and a final hymn. In this English edition the hymns and prayers have been omitted. Von Holst's expositions with their vivid detail – sometimes imaginative and sometimes based on historic research – will draw readers into a deep contemplation of Christ's suffering and urge them to accept Jesus into their hearts.

Emmy Barth Maendel

The Days of Preparation

Ash Wednesday
to Saturday

Ash Wednesday Morning

The Lamb of God

The next day [John the Baptist] saw Jesus coming toward him, and said, "Behold, the Lamb of God, who takes away the sin of the world!"

John 1:29

"**BEHOLD, THE FIRE AND THE WOOD,** but where is the lamb for a burnt offering?" Isaac asked his father, Abraham, on that strange journey (Gen. 22:7). His father answered, deeply moved, "God will provide for himself the lamb." But the lamb that God the Lord would in fact provide as a sacrifice for the lost world was described in this way by the prophet Isaiah: "He was oppressed and he was afflicted, yet he opened not his mouth; like a lamb that is led to the slaughter, and like a sheep that before its shearers is silent, so he opened not his mouth" (Isa. 53:7).

Now John the Baptist stands in the fertile Jordan Valley. Light glows in his eyes, and lightning flashes from his preaching. His disciples surround him and very mixed throngs of people listen to his words.

Suddenly he is silent. Jesus of Nazareth, at that time still an unknown man, walks into the crowd's sight. John looks at him. The Spirit of God comes over him, and he recognizes in the simple wanderer the Messiah, promised and looked for with longing hearts for thousands of years, the servant of Jehovah, the Lamb of God.

Overwhelmed by this recognition, John points to the approaching man and calls out the momentous words, "Behold, the Lamb of God who takes away the sin of the world!" This utterance has made him the greatest of the prophets. What depth there is in these words! John grasps the divine mission of Jesus and his innermost nature, will, and work. He looks into the heart of God and into the opened heavens, but he also sees the curse of humankind's sin. He sees this burden laid upon the shoulders of this one man, who bears it and takes it away by his atoning death – and so sets the lost world free and founds a new, transfigured world.

Yes, this Jesus is the pure lamb. No one can accuse him of any sin, and the Father himself bears witness, "This is my beloved Son, with whom I am well pleased"

(Matt. 3:17). He is also the patient lamb, for he was obedient unto death, even to death on the cross. He is the gentle lamb, for while bleeding on the cross, he prays that his enemies may be forgiven. In everything he is the Lamb of God, the holy sacrificial lamb, through whom all who believe in him will be perfected in eternity.

This Lamb of God is our Jesus Christ, our Redeemer and Savior, who loves us too with his eternal love. He suffered and died for us too, in order to make us blessed. Shouldn't we love him in return? Shouldn't we be grateful to him and faithfully follow him?

Today the time of celebrating the memory of his suffering and death begins. Will this Lenten season be a blessing to us? How often have we already lived through it, and how often has it passed by! Perhaps it now comes to us for the last time. Shall we die without taking the Lamb of God into our hearts? May God in his grace preserve us from that. May he overcome all the resistance of our old nature and bless this time of Lent for our eternal salvation.

2

Ash Wednesday Evening

Who Takes Away
the Sin of the World

*Behold, the Lamb of God, who takes away the sin of the
world!*

John 1:29

THIS TESTIMONY of John's is the heart and the star
of the whole gospel. It is true, John's mouth was soon
closed by a bloody death, but the apostles proclaimed
it further: "Behold, the Lamb of God, who takes away
the sin of the world!" They too have died, but this
gospel rings through all centuries and hallows them.
And when today the church of the Lord gathers to celebrate the Holy Supper, she looks up to the Crucified
One and thousands of voices sing, "O Lamb of God,
who bears the sin of the world, have mercy on us and
give us your peace!"

We are often weighed down with our work, our cares and suffering, but if we had to bear the full weight of our sin and guilt, we would sink under it into eternal night. The beam of the cross that the Lord carried to Golgotha on his torn and bleeding shoulders was heavy, but the invisible burden that rested on that cursed wood was heavier. It was not the sin of one man that was laid on the Lamb of God, but of all people – truly, the sin, guilt, and death penalty of the whole world. The season of Lent admonishes us to look well at this Lamb, and John exhorts us with his challenge, "Behold."

Just as once the children of Israel in the wilderness, seeking help from the bites of fierce snakes, looked up to the bronze serpent, so we too would look to the Crucified One, who bore our burden and atoned for our guilt. We would look to him with ever fuller, ever deeper and more grateful faith. But for this, new and pure eyes are necessary. We must beg the Lord for these if we want to grasp our Redeemer's suffering in the depths of our hearts.

With such eyes, my soul, contemplate your suffering Savior. See him in the garden of Gethsemane in the shadow of night, lying prostrate on his face, struggling with death and sweating drops of blood. See him in the judgment hall, bearing in silence the lashes of the cruel executioner, enduring spitting and a crown of thorns. Take your place below the cross at Golgotha and hear the seven last words of the dying man. Look at the bloody wounds on his head, his limbs quivering with pain, his eyes filled with tears.

Look still deeper: look into the heart of Jesus and see his obedience to his Father and his compassion for you. See his heart break and his head bowed in death. Look until your heart also breaks in pain and love, and your eyes overflow with tears of gratitude. All who look at him and bear him in their souls like this together form the great invisible church of God here on earth, which will be revealed on the day of glory. She will see this Lamb again as her glorified, eternal king. Then she will experience the prophecy of the new covenant: "The Lamb in the midst of the throne will be their shepherd, and he will guide them to springs of living water, and God will wipe away every tear from their eyes" (Rev. 7:17).

3

Thursday Morning

The Lord's Road

And taking the twelve, he said to them, "See, we are going
up to Jerusalem, and everything that is written about the
Son of Man by the prophets will be accomplished. For he will
be delivered over to the Gentiles and will be mocked and
shamefully treated and spit upon. And after flogging him,
they will kill him, and on the third day he will rise."

Luke 18:31–33

AS LONG AS THE TEMPLE OF JEHOVAH was standing in Jerusalem and the beautiful services of the Lord
were celebrated there, every year when spring came and
the Passover festival was drawing near, the joyful cry
rang out, "We are going up to Jerusalem!" It resounded
in all the towns and villages, cottages and palaces of
the Holy Land. When Jesus went to the festival for
the first time with his parents as a twelve-year-old boy,
how joyfully it rang in his soul: "We are going up to

Jerusalem!" This continued throughout his earthy walk to the first years of his mission.

How different in content and tone this call sounds in today's text. Jesus was on his last journey and, accompanied by his disciples, came from the land on the east side of the Jordan into the southern Jordan Valley on the great military road that led to Jericho. This was the most beautiful and most fertile region in the whole land. The road led through avenues of palm trees, rose gardens, and fragrant fields. It was spring once more and the Passover was again near. Everything was green and in bloom; aromatic scents filled the air. Throngs of joyful pilgrims passed them from all directions. The pinnacles of Jericho glittered as they drew near. The road to Jerusalem, situated on the holy hill only a six-hour walk away, led through this town.

"We are going up to Jerusalem!" rang joyfully in the hearts of the pilgrims, and the Lord's disciples and friends were filled with hope. They expected that there he would triumph at long last over the horde of the mighty and embittered foe and gloriously establish his kingdom. The Lord also said to his disciples these words, "We are going up to Jerusalem" – but what did he add? "The Son of Man will be delivered over to the Gentiles and will be mocked and shamefully treated and spit upon. And after flogging him, they will kill him, and on the third day he will rise."

This pilgrimage was the road to his suffering and death, and he walked it with unflinching faithfulness. For his heart glowed with love for his Jerusalem. It was the city of the great king, his anointed ancestor David, and it was the city of the great God, his heavenly Father.

His soul was filled with deep sadness: "Jerusalem, Jerusalem, the city that kills the prophets and stones those who are sent to it! How often would I have gathered your children together as a hen gathers her brood under her wings, and you were not willing!" (Matt. 23:37) Since he could do nothing else for his royal city, he wanted to die in her and for her. His road to the heavenly Jerusalem for which he longed passed through this earthly, doomed Jerusalem. There is no city on earth today that has the significance of the old Jerusalem – but we yearn for the heavenly one of which we sing.

4

Thursday Evening

The Disciples' Road

And taking the twelve, he said to them, "See, we are going up to Jerusalem, and everything that is written about the Son of Man by the prophets will be accomplished. For he will be delivered over to the Gentiles and will be mocked and shamefully treated and spit upon. And after flogging him, they will kill him, and on the third day he will rise." But they understood none of these things. This saying was hidden from them, and they did not grasp what was said.

Luke 18:31–34

WHEN THE LORD TOLD THEM what he would have to suffer, the souls of his listeners were stunned as if by a thunderclap. "But they understood none of these things. This saying was hidden from them, and they did not grasp what was said." They heard but did not understand; they saw but did not perceive (Mark 4:12). They understood nothing of the Lord's thoughts because they were full of their own ideas. They did not want to hear of suffering and death, for they were dreaming of happiness and glory. They saw in their mind's eye the dawning glory of the Messiah's kingdom with its proclamation of healing and salvation. They thought that what the Master was saying about shame, suffering, and death must be some kind of parable, meaning something quite different from the actual words. They felt only one thing: that there was something terribly oppressive in the Lord's words, so they continued on their way with him, half-stunned.

But the Lord knew exactly what was awaiting him. He foresaw the shadows of Gethsemane and felt the horror of the cross on Golgotha. He had the power to turn back at each step and return to his Father's glory, yet he went forward. What was it that urged him to go this way to the end? It was obedience to his Father's will, compassionate love toward the lost world. So he strode on to his bloody death, but in his heart he bore the comfort of a victorious resurrection. And wherever he went and wherever he stayed, heavenly blessing lay on his work – such as the blind man who was healed by his faith (Mark 10:52) and the salvation that came to Zacchaeus (Luke 19:9).

But the Lord did not say, "I am going up to Jerusalem." He said, "We are going." It is this "we" that we have to emphasize. For it does not apply only to those first disciples; it also applies to us insofar as we want to be his followers. For us, too, the way to glory passes through suffering and death. To suffer with Christ for sin in the obedience of faith; to give up all foolish wishes and vain hopes with our eyes fixed on him; with him and in love to him to give our old self up to death; to die with him in quiet confidence in a blessed resurrection when our last hour comes; and then to be with him forever in the heavenly Jerusalem – this is our task.

If a stranger should ask us on our pilgrim way, "Where are you going?" then our whole life and being should answer, "We are going up to Jerusalem." When young people are accepted into the church and then have to face the world, when newlyweds begin their married life together, when men or women are given a new task – they should say to themselves, "We are going up to Jerusalem." Not only at this season of Lent when we accompany our Lord on his way to suffering and the cross, but throughout our whole walk on this earth, both in the springtime and in the winter of life, may this remain our watchword: "We are going up to Jerusalem."

5

Friday Morning

The Fire of the Spirit and the Baptism of Suffering

I came to cast fire on the earth, and would that it were already kindled! I have a baptism to be baptized with, and how great is my distress until it is accomplished!

Luke 12:49–50

WHAT KIND OF FIRE does Christ want to kindle on earth? It is the fire of the Holy Spirit, as John the Baptist already prophesied, "He who is coming after me will baptize you with the Holy Spirit and with fire" (Matt. 3:11). Accordingly, the Holy Spirit came on the Day of Pentecost in tongues of fire. This fire has a consuming power to begin with. It is a fire that causes dissension and struggle, and the Lord throws it into the sinner's breast to awake him from sleep and death. As he said, "I have not come to bring peace, but a sword" (Matt. 10:34). For it consumes darkness, sin, and destruction.

That is why all who want to continue in the rotten state of this world hate it, and it gives rise to a fierce battle against the disciples of the Lord. But where its consuming power has stood the test, it also becomes a fire of joy and blessing. It enlightens the hearts of believers and leads them to know God. It purifies their souls from sin and guilt and raises them to a life of communion with God. Its holy flames mount to the Father of Light as worshiping love and burn in selfless dedication in serving others. Where this fire is burning, it is heaven on earth. The disciples on the road to Emmaus felt it when they said, "Did not our hearts burn within us while he talked to us on the road?" (Luke 24:32).

Now, when the Lord called out on his last journey, "Would that it were already kindled!" he gave his disciples a deep insight into his heart and soul. He bears this fire within himself, and he knows that it must be kindled in others. He sees it burning in the breast of his disciples, spreading from heart to heart, from nation to nation, a fiery sign flaming from century to century. Yes, he sees at last the new heaven and the new earth in this element of the eternal light. An intense longing for that time lays hold of him.

But now a deep sadness casts itself between his longing and its fulfillment. What a fight must still be fought, what a sacrifice must still be made, before his task is fulfilled! That is why he says, "I have a baptism to be baptized with, and how great is my distress until it is accomplished!" A terrible flood surges up against the holy fire – the flood of his suffering, of his death. This is his baptism, his baptism of blood. He knows what awaits him, but he goes straight into it in the strength of love. And he is not ashamed to admit his apprehension. "How great is my distress!" he says.

We are deeply moved when he speaks. We are filled with wonder when he heals the sick, awakens the dead, and calms the stormy waves. We will fall on our knees before him in worship when we see him one day as judge of the world. But when the heavenly hero is afraid, when his soul trembles, when he pours out his anguish, seeking comfort in his disciples, even hard hearts must become soft. We must call out, "Yes, you are ours, and we are yours!" When this happens, his fire is already kindled.

6

Friday Evening

Humble Yourself, My Heart

Then the mother of the sons of Zebedee came up to him with her sons, and kneeling before him she asked him for something. And he said to her, "What do you want?" She said to him, "Say that these two sons of mine are to sit, one at your right hand and one at your left, in your kingdom." Jesus answered, "You do not know what you are asking. Are you able to drink the cup that I am to drink?" They said to him, "We are able." He said to them, "You will drink my cup, but to sit at my right hand and at my left is not mine to grant, but it is for those for whom it has been prepared by my Father."

Matthew 20:20–23

IT WAS A GREAT-HEARTED REQUEST that John and James made through their mother, Salome, to their Master. The thought was a noble one that considered all places of honor beside earthly kings as nothing in comparison with a seat of honor at Jesus' side. The faith was great: that the glory of the humble Son of Man, in spite of all that he had said about suffering, would soon surpass all human grandeur. The love was ardent, seeking no more blessed goal than to stay beside the Lord forever. A noble courage was needed to dare to ask for such a thing. Yet in spite of all this, an alien fire burned in this request of the Sons of Thunder, for it also contained a forward vanity, a thoughtless pride, and a human messianic hope. So with gentle dignity the Lord rebuked them: "You do not know what you are asking," and held before their eyes the cup that he would have to drink and the baptism that he would have to undergo. Thus he reminded them in two pictures of the suffering and death facing him.

Just as once the waters of the Jordan (beside whose banks they were now standing) had been poured over him at his baptism on beginning his mission, now the dark waves of outward suffering were to flood over him. Just as the precious contents of the wine glass must be savored to the full, so he must take the wine of tribulation and accept it inwardly. He must drain God's cup of wrath in humble submission if the Father's counsel is to be carried out. In this way the Lord wants to impress deeply upon them the fundamental principle of his kingdom: greatness only through humility; sovereignty only through service; the crown only through the cross. Whoever wants to ascend with Jesus must first descend with him.

The deep-going question of conscience that Jesus asked – if they could drink his cup and endure his baptism – was answered by both disciples in rash self-confidence, but also in daring truthfulness, with a joyful "Yes!" Later they both honored this "Yes" – John through a long life filled with suffering in faithful service of the Lord, and James through his early, bloody death.

No one can be a Christian without the cross. The closer we would be to the Lord, the deeper we have to go with him, outwardly or inwardly, into his humiliation and into his suffering. That is essential. So let the Lord's question pierce deeply into your conscience, my soul: Can you, will you drink his cup? Will you endure his baptism? Blessed are all who, through life and death, can humbly answer, "Yes."

7

Saturday Morning

The Enemies Gather

So the chief priests and the Pharisees gathered the council and said, "What are we to do? For this man performs many signs. If we let him go on like this, everyone will believe in him, and the Romans will come and take away both our place and our nation."

John 11:47–48

EVER SINCE the Lord's first appearance, he encountered malicious opposition from the Pharisees and elders. The higher the sun of his activity rose, the deeper grew their hostility. For he had nothing in common with them, nor they with him. They wanted a brilliant, political messianic kingdom; he demanded repentance and a change of heart. They looked for pleasure and power; he demanded obedience and surrendered faith in his divine mission. Thus their hostility rose to the point of murderous hatred. Already when he had been in Jerusalem previously, they had wanted to stone him. He had escaped their clutches at that time, for his hour had not yet come, and he still wanted to allow them a time of grace. Then suddenly he appeared once more before the gates of the royal city in quiet Bethany, where by raising Lazarus his divine majesty was made to shine more gloriously than ever through the garment of lowliness. This deed was a powerful sermon without words, addressed to his nation; it was the last shaking call to his city: "Awake, Jerusalem!" If she did not grasp this last warning, there was nothing for it but that judgment should break in.

The raising of Lazarus roused tremendous excitement in the people, and many believed in the divine victor over death. But that very fact fanned the hatred, which the ruling classes had nursed for so long, to fanatical rage. A meeting of the council was held, and while the Lord was by the Jordan preparing to drink the cup of suffering, here in the den of hatred the poisoned drink was made ready for him. "What should we do?" asked the elders of Israel. But these men did not ask in order to discover the truth but in order to suppress it; they did not ask in order to find God's will but in order to force through their own wicked will. They admit: "This man performs many signs; everyone will believe in him." But instead of hastening to him and placing their hearts and lives at his service in adoration, they consider how to cause his downfall. They do this only to maintain their own influence over the people and so defy the hated Romans in their own way.

It happens still today that human hearts and political parties, filled with passionate hatred, stifle the voice of truth and conscience to find a favorable opportunity for a crime they have already decided on. But we want to flee from such purpose as from the plague. We would rather suffer and die with the Lord than live and rule without him or against him.

8

Saturday Evening

The High Priest's Counsel

But one of them, Caiaphas, who was high priest that year,
said to them, "You know nothing at all. Nor do you under-
stand that it is better for you that one man should die for the
people, not that the whole nation should perish."

John 11:49–50

THERE IN THE MEETING of the council a pertinent
answer is found to the question, "What are we to do?"
Caiaphas, the High Priest, listened for a long time
to the excited speeches. Now he rose and said, "You
know nothing at all. Nor do you understand that it is
better for you that one man should die for the people,
not that the whole nation should perish." Some of the
council may have secretly had the same thought but
not dared to express it openly. Caiaphas, however,
shies away from nothing. It is all one to him whether
they do right or wrong, whether they fulfill the law

or bring bloodguilt upon themselves. His decision is certain. Earthly power must be secured even if heaven is lost in the process. If the agitated populace is to be restored to order and the authority of those in power maintained, then Christ has to die. That is the radical expedient. As always in such meetings, strength prevails. Caiaphas's suggestion forces its way through, and the most terrible crime of the human race, the murder of the Messiah, is decided.

The whole meaning and purpose of this murderous decision can be summed up in Caiaphas's remark: one for all. Yet "one for all" rang also in the shining depth of the heart of God. Caiaphas had to prophesy because he was the high priest. Without knowing or wanting it, he had to disclose God's eternal counsel of grace. All people have sinned and deserve death, but God will not let himself be robbed of his most beloved creation by Satan's power and cunning. His heart is filled with pity for the whole race of his lost children. For this reason he prepared the one who is the head of all. He alone is pure and has done nothing to deserve death. Nevertheless he wants to die for all, for he is love. He is able to die without perishing, because he is life. His death is valid for all in the sight of eternal justice, because he is more than all, and because all are one in him. If he dies, all have died in his death; if he lives, all live in him. This is Jesus of Nazareth, God's Son and the Son of Man.

One for all – that is now the comfort of all who have faith. What a dark mystery life and death would be without this word! But if the inscription "one for all" is placed over the manger and the cross, how clear everything becomes.

How could we dare to call ourselves God's children if Christ were not born for us? How could we believe in the forgiveness of our sins if he had not atoned for us? How could we approach death with tranquil hearts if he had not died for us? Yes, "Christ for us" – "One for all." That is the great fact of salvation through which the world is saved, our human race is newborn, our life is blessed, and death is overcome. Whoever grasps this One in faith has everything that he needs both here and in eternity, peace on earth and blessedness in heaven.

First Week of Lent

9

Sunday Morning

The Anointing

Six days before the Passover, Jesus therefore came to Bethany, where Lazarus was, whom Jesus had raised from the dead. So they gave a dinner for him in the house of Simon the leper. Martha served, and Lazarus was one of those reclining with him at table. Mary therefore took a flask of expensive ointment made from pure nard, and poured it on Jesus' head as he reclined at table, and anointed his feet and wiped them with her hair. The house was filled with the fragrance of the perfume.

John 12:1–3

THE LORD WAS ON HIS LAST JOURNEY from Jericho, the city of roses, to the peaceful little village of Bethany, whose name means "house of palms," situated on the Mount of Olives just an hour's walk from Jerusalem. There, on the Saturday before Palm Sunday, Simon the leper had a feast prepared in his honor. This act of hospitality and joyous acknowledgment of Jesus required courage, for the council had already issued a warrant for the Lord's arrest (John 11:57). But at this supper he was safe and surrounded by grateful love.

The circle included the host, whom he had healed of leprosy; Lazarus, whom he had raised from the dead; the disciples, whom he had chosen; and Mary and Martha, who so gladly served him. Here the Lord was granted a short time of peace and quiet with his own before the outbreak of the last storm. But the joy of the company was dampened by vague forebodings aroused by what the Lord had said about his suffering and the obvious plots of the enemy.

Mary in particular was seized with melancholy, and her love rose to its highest peak. She had with her a costly treasure, an alabaster flask filled with oil of nard. At the urge of her love she broke the glass and poured the ethereal contents over the head and feet of her Savior. In doing this she also broke the outward forms of womanly reserve in order to envelop him completely in the fragrance of her love. He had anointed her soul with the words of his spirit; she anointed his head with the nard of her love. He had dried her tears at her brother's grave; she dried his feet with her hair.

Wherever believing souls gather in unanimity today, thanking him in loving gratitude that they have been cleansed from the leprosy of sin and saved from the jaws of death, they experience Bethany. The Lord is in their midst and blesses their fellowship with his peace-bringing presence. But where are the souls like Mary, who break the heart of their old nature and joyfully give everything they have in the service of his love? The Lord knows them and sees them blossoming in the valley of humility, where they are mostly quiet and hidden, offering the strength and beauty of their lives in gratitude to their Redeemer and in service to others. Indeed the church, the bride of the Lord, is herself such a Mary when she remembers his passion in little family circles or in large church gatherings and accompanies him on his way to the cross with faith and reverence, adoration and prayer.

10

Sunday Evening

Mary Is Justified

But Judas Iscariot, one of his disciples (he who was about to betray him), said, "Why was this ointment not sold for three hundred denarii and given to the poor?" But Judas said this, not because he cared about the poor, but because he was a thief, and having charge of the moneybag he used to help himself to what was put into it.

There were some who said to themselves indignantly, "Why was the ointment wasted like that? For this ointment could have been sold for more than three hundred denarii and given to the poor." And they scolded her. But Jesus said, "Leave her alone. Why do you trouble her? She has done a beautiful thing to me. For you always have the poor with you, and whenever you want, you can do good for them. But you will not always have me. She has done what she could; she has anointed my body beforehand for burial. And truly, I say to you, wherever the gospel is proclaimed in the whole world, what she has done will be told in memory of her."

John 12:4–6; Mark 14:4–9

HERE FOR THE FIRST TIME we are given a glimpse into the dark abyss of Judas's heart. The Lord's repeated references to his suffering had gradually made it clear to Judas that this Jesus would not establish the dreamed-of messianic kingdom in worldly glory, that following him would not lead to the expected riches and honors. He walked beside his Master, brooding in silence, while within him the love of money grew to thieving avarice, and under the reproachful looks and words of the Lord, his selfishness hardened into hatred of Christ. It is true, he still wore the mask of discipleship, but he was incapable of understanding the love that urged Mary. Yet he felt judged in his heart for his stone-hard egotism by her act of dedication, and the poison of his malice burst forth. This attitude of Judas reveals for all time the mystery of the hatred of the world for the church of Christ. The Lord's enemies feel rebuked by the behavior of his true disciples and so try to get rid of them.

Judas tried in vain to cover his rage with the cloak of cleverly calculated love to the poor. It is true that some of the disciples were thoughtless and foolish enough to agree with him, but the Lord saw through him. He brought Mary's act of love into the brightest light by saying, "Leave her alone. Why do you trouble her? She has done what she could; she has done a beautiful thing to me." Oh that we might also receive his praise: "You have done what you could!" Truly, it is little that we can do, but who has really done even the little he can? Won't our bitterest self-accusations one day be that we have not done what we could? But where perfect love is at work, it does everything it can. And where it does, the Lord himself adds to it far more than we can imagine or understand. He accepts Mary's loving deed as the anointing of his holy body for its burial and resurrection, and declares that this will be proclaimed by every tongue as long as the world exists. When we refresh someone who is thirsty with a drink of cool water, he looks upon it as done to himself (Matt. 25:35, 40). When we try to do God's will, urged by love, he says these efforts fulfill the law: "Love is the fulfilling of the law (Rom. 13:10).

At the Last Judgment all calculating egotists (however hypocritically they still know how to cry, "Lord! Lord!") will be ordered away with the words, "Depart from me, you cursed" (Matt. 25:41). But those who have lived and died in love will hear the gracious words: "You have done what you could. Enter into the joy of your master" (Matt. 25:23).

11

Monday Morning

The King Enters Jerusalem

The next day the large crowd that had come to the feast heard that Jesus was coming to Jerusalem. So they took branches of palm trees and went out to meet him . . . Jesus found a young donkey and sat on it.

And many spread their cloaks on the road, and others spread leafy branches that they had cut from the fields. And those who went before and those who followed were shouting, "Hosanna! Blessed is he who comes in the name of the Lord! Blessed is the coming kingdom of our father David! Hosanna in the highest!"

As he was drawing near—already on the way down the Mount of Olives—the whole multitude of his disciples began to rejoice and praise God with a loud voice for all the mighty works that they had seen, saying, "Blessed is the King who comes in the name of the Lord! Peace in heaven and glory in the highest!" And some of the Pharisees in the crowd said to

him, "Teacher, rebuke your disciples." He answered, "I tell
you, if these were silent, the very stones would cry out."

John 12:12–14; Mark 11:8–10; Luke 19:37–40

WHILE THE LORD WAS IN QUIET BETHANY there
was tremendous excitement in Jerusalem. Hundreds of
thousands of pilgrims had come to celebrate the Passover, and the royal city, which was already crowded, was
filled to overflowing. One question filled the thoughts
and conversations of all: Will the prophet of Nazareth,
the great conqueror of death whom the council excom-
municated, also come to the festival? Will he dare to do
so? Then the news spread rapidly that he was already in
Bethany and was preparing to enter Jerusalem.

His enemies were enraged, his followers encouraged,
the indifferent were roused, and great and very mixed
crowds set off for the Mount of Olives and waited for
him in tense excitement. The cry rang out: "There he
is!" The King of Peace came into sight at the top of the
hill riding on a donkey, surrounded by his disciples and
many other followers. At the sight of him, reverence
for this wonderful man of God, which was repressed
till now, breaks forth with irresistible power in the

crowded throng. They recognize him as the promised Son of David, the longed-for Messiah King. They spread their clothes in his path, break green branches from the palm trees and wave them joyfully in the air. In this way they receive and accompany their great yet so unassuming King. An enthusiasm from above takes possession of their souls. They begin to sing songs of praise: "Hosanna to the Son of David! Blessed is he who comes in the name of the Lord! Hosanna in the highest!" These psalms spread from one throng to another: "Blessed is the coming kingdom of our father David! Blessed is the king who comes in the name of the Lord!"

The enthusiastic singing continues to ring out more and more powerfully right up to the gates of the capital city – indeed, right up into the temple precincts: "Hosanna to the king of Israel! Peace in heaven and glory in the highest!"

What a blessing might have dawned upon Israel that day if the whole nation had paid homage to its king and been faithful to him unto death! But the higher the waves of the people's joy rise, the fiercer grows the hatred of the enemies. Standing by the roadside, they call out to the Lord in their exasperation, "Teacher, rebuke your disciples." He, however, accepts the people's homage and rebuts these grim elders with the words, "If these were silent, the very stones would cry out."

But the populace is fickle while the hatred of the adversary remains firm. The king enters his city, but his crown will be a crown of thorns, and his throne the cross on Golgotha.

How do you, my soul, honor your King? How are you, his church, accompanying your Savior on his way to death? How are you keeping your pledge of loyalty?

12

Monday Evening

Immanuel's Tears

And when he drew near and saw the city, he wept over it, saying, "Would that you, even you, had known on this day the things that make for peace! But now they are hidden from your eyes. For the days will come upon you, when your enemies will set up a barricade around you and surround you and hem you in on every side and tear you down to the ground, you and your children within you. And they will not leave one stone upon another in you, because you did not know the time of your visitation."

Luke 19:41–44

WHEN THE LORD had reached the top of the Mount of Olives, the royal city with the gleaming gold of the temple lay in all its glory before his eyes. But in the midst of the disciples and rejoicing throngs around him, a deep sadness filled his holy soul at this sight, and his eyes overflowed with tears.

If a child weeps, we feel pity; if a hero weeps, our hearts are unnerved. But when Jesus weeps, Jesus the Son of God and of man, the lion of the tribe of Judah, it brings us to our knees, and we fearfully have to ask, "What is the cause of such tears?" The Lord himself answers us in words of deep emotion. He is not weeping for himself. He is not weeping because of his own approaching suffering. He represses these feelings. They are tears of love and sorrow that he sheds for his unhappy Jerusalem. He knows that there is still a time of grace for Jerusalem, that she may still be saved and raised to her true glory if at the last moment she turns with her whole heart to the Messiah who is just entering her. But he also sees Jerusalem's hardness of heart. He sees how she rejects her only helper and savior, and that because of this the storm clouds of God's judgment gather ever more darkly over the beloved city. He sees her at last, broken and ruined by the iron military power of the pagan Romans, sinking in smoke and rubble.

Jesus' tears also have significance for us. He weeps for us, too, as long as we rush unrepentant along the broad way that leads to destruction. The tears of a mother for her morally corrupt child ought to wake him out of his sleep of sin. The tears of Immanuel ought to fall into our sinful hearts like drops of smelted gold, burning, startling, and shaking us up.

How many nations are still blinded like Jerusalem of old! They build their houses and palaces and set up their governments without fear of God and without prayer, obstinately relying on their own strength. They do not see God's approaching judgment; they do not feel the quaking of the earth under their feet; they reject all admonitions to repent and turn around. How many people who call themselves Christians, even the old and infirm, do not see their death coming! They do not make use of the time of grace still given them; they do not lay hold of the one who alone can save them and make them blessed. Oh, that the tears of Jesus' love may still move us all, before it is too late, to consider what gives true peace.

13

Tuesday Morning

The Grain of Wheat

Now among those who went up to worship at the feast were some Greeks. So these came to Philip, who was from Beth-saida in Galilee, and asked him, "Sir, we wish to see Jesus." Philip went and told Andrew; Andrew and Philip went and told Jesus. And Jesus answered them, "The hour has come for the Son of Man to be glorified. Truly, truly, I say to you, unless a grain of wheat falls into the earth and dies, it remains alone; but if it dies, it bears much fruit. Whoever loves his life loses it, and whoever hates his life in this world will keep it for eternal life. If anyone serves me, he must follow me; and where I am, there will my servant be also. If anyone serves me, the Father will honor him."

John 12:20–26

WHEN THE LORD HAD ENTERED the forecourt of the temple after his solemn entry into Jerusalem, some Greeks also wanted to see Jesus. Just as after his birth the wise men from the east approached him, so now before his death these Greeks come as representatives of the nations of the world. Moved by the news of the raising of Lazarus, struck by the jubilation of the surging crowd, they expressed their wish to see the Lord – the very deep and mostly unconscious longing of all pagans and indeed of the whole human race.

Jesus himself saw in their coming the beginning of his future glorification, which was to reveal him not only as Israel's Messiah but also as the head and savior of all nations. At the same time in the parable of the grain of wheat, he taught his hearers that his way to glory could only be through death. As at dawn the light of the coming day blends with the darkness of the night, here the Lord's sadness over his approaching death was interwoven with the joyful hope of resurrection.

In the parable of the grain of wheat he points to Golgotha and the tomb in Joseph's garden. When the divine grain of wheat was buried, his disciples surely thought of these words and began to sense something of their meaning. But it was also for us that the Lord went this way, and we should now go with him: that is, we should die with him, crucify our old nature at his cross, and finally sink into the earth, trusting in him. But our dying should also be illuminated by the assurance of a blessed resurrection.

43

In spring the grain of wheat that was sown awakens to new life, and all the other young blades of wheat shine with it in fresh green. They ripen and bear fruit in the light of the sun. It is the same with the highest form of nature: humankind. We also can only attain to new and more beautiful life through death and the grave. Even though the winter is long, the day of resurrection must come when this human seed, buried with so many tears, will awaken and bloom. The resurrection of Jesus Christ is our guarantee for this. If this heavenly grain of wheat had not fallen into the earth and died, then Christ would have remained alone, the unique God-man, highly exalted, apart from and above all other humans. But now, since he has died and risen from the dead, he bears fruit many thousandfold. All of us who live on earth as his redeemed, the church in whom he lives, gathered from all nations, and the countless hosts of the blessed in the heavenly paradise – all form the one nation, the one body of the Lord, the blessed fruit of his resurrection. And when finally spring comes and Easter morning dawns for those whose bodies rest in the earth, when they are raised in eternal transfiguration to live on the new earth under the new heaven, then the Lord Jesus Christ will be the sun that illuminates them and he will be glorified in all.

14

Tuesday Evening

When I Am Lifted Up

"And I, when I am lifted up from the earth, will draw all people to myself." He said this to show by what kind of death he was going to die.

John 12:32–33

THE LORD SPOKE THIS WORD about his being lifted up to the Jewish people and to the seeking Greeks shortly after he had entered the temple forecourt. What he meant here by his "lifting up" is explained not only by John's addition, "This he said to indicate the kind of death he was to die," but also by what the Lord himself said to Nicodemus, "And just as Moses lifted up the serpent in the wilderness, so must the Son of Man be lifted up" (John 3:14).

In contrast to the lifting up desired by the disciples and the populace (that is, being raised to the royal throne of a worldly monarchy) the Lord here envisages being lifted up on the cross, where in his sacrificial death he was to bear the whole curse that the serpent had brought upon the human race. Nevertheless, just as the foot of the cross was rooted in the earth while its head was raised to heaven, he was to die only in order to be raised to the throne of heavenly majesty through overcoming death and bursting the grave. Thus he combines in one prophetic saying his being lifted up on the cross and his elevation to glory.

"I will draw all people to myself" means he will not coerce with outward force but draw them with the gentle yet world-vanquishing might of his sacrificial love that bears all things and suffers all things. He will not terrify them with threats and punishments, but win them through wakening a free inner conviction, through kindling a holy love for him.

In this way Christ draws Jews and Greeks – all peoples and all nations who allow themselves to be drawn – out of the bonds of earth to himself on the cross. His love overcomes their natural opposition, enduring, atoning, and forgiving. In his suffering he becomes the most beautiful man in the eyes of all repentant sinners. At the foot of his cross the old heart dies; at the foot of his cross a new heart is born. Thus he drew the criminal to himself. "To myself," says the

Lord – not to any kind of dogma, not to a law, but to himself, to his most holy person.

He draws them into his discipleship, into his school of the cross, into a God-fearing attitude of mind, and so makes them living members of his church on earth. Finally he draws his own, through death, out of the prison of the body, out of this earth's vale of tears, up to the perfect life and love of his heavenly kingdom. There they will experience the meaning of the divine prophecy: "I have loved you with an everlasting love; therefore I have drawn you to myself" (Jer. 31:3).

15

Judas's Bargain

*Then one of the twelve, whose name was Judas Iscariot,
went to the chief priests and said, "What will you give me if
I deliver him over to you?" And they paid him thirty pieces
of silver. And from that moment he sought an opportunity
to betray him.*

Matthew 26:14–16

IS IT TRUE that each Christian has a price for which
he would sell his Savior? Unfortunately it is only too
true in the case of all who are not willing to break with
sin. It is true for those whose Christianity only serves
to satisfy their earthly desires, or who imagine they are
able to combine it with serving the world. We see what
this must lead to in the shattering example of Judas.

The closer his relationship with the Lord, the more
powerfully did he feel himself compelled to make
a quick decision between complete dedication and

hostile desertion. Since he did not want to tear his deeply rooted love of self and of the world out of his heart, he was dragged into the camp of the enemy. For the miserable price of a slave, for thirty silver pieces, the once enthusiastic disciple sold his Master! To be sure, the paltry silver pieces were not the real object of his action. Above all he sought to rid himself of this master, who by his constant demand for a complete change of heart and life had become ever more unbearable to him. He sought to acquire a reputation in the eyes of the leaders of his nation and so reach once more a comfortable position in life. Incidentally, his avaricious nature was not averse to making a small profit while doing so. While considering these thoughts, his better self rose up once more against them. Once more a terrible struggle was fought in his breast, but with the sad result that his conscience was finally crushed. Then he went and concluded the hellish agreement.

But the king of heaven and earth, in whose light and love the transfigured earth will one day celebrate its eternal Sabbath, was valued at the paltry price of a slave. What humiliation and outrage he had to endure! He emptied himself and took the form of a servant, and was obedient unto death. Surely he has borne our griefs and carried our sorrows. He atoned for our pride and suffered our humiliation. Upon him was the chastisement that brought us peace (Isa. 53:4–5).

But for those of his disciples who thank him from their hearts, who willingly empty themselves of self with him, who break completely with their sin and take upon themselves the form of a servant in devotion to their Master – in short, those who truly believe in him and love him above everything – for them there is no Judas-price in any world for which they might forsake and betray their Savior. History bears witness to this in the joyful death of countless martyrs, who were able to say to their Lord and Master with the psalmist: "Whom have I in heaven but you? And there is nothing on earth that I desire besides you. My flesh and my heart may fail, but God is the strength of my heart and my portion forever" (Ps. 73:25–26).

How do you stand, my soul, with regard to your sins and to the selling price? Examine yourself carefully. Whoever loves his life will lose it, but whoever loses it for Christ's sake will keep it (John 12:25).

16

Wednesday Evening

The Fig Tree

In the morning, as he was returning to the city, he became hungry. And seeing a fig tree by the wayside, he went to it and found nothing on it but only leaves. And he said to it, "May no fruit ever come from you again!" And the fig tree withered at once. When the disciples saw it, they marveled, saying, "How did the fig tree wither at once?" And Jesus answered them, "Truly, I say to you, if you have faith and do not doubt, you will not only do what has been done to the fig tree, but even if you say to this mountain, 'Be taken up and thrown into the sea,' it will happen. And whatever you ask in prayer, you will receive, if you have faith."

Matthew 21:18–22

AFTER THE LORD had made his entry into Jerusalem, cleansed the temple, spoken powerful words to the people, and healed the blind and the lame (conscious all the time of the wrath of his enemies), he returned in the evening to peaceful Bethany. The next morning he returned to the royal city. His soul was filled with sorrowful thoughts as he walked with his disciples through the fig grove of Bethphage, and the pinnacles of the lost city rose again before his eyes. Most of the crowd who had hailed him on Palm Sunday were pilgrims coming to the festival; the citizens of Jerusalem itself were mostly hostile to the Lord, under the influence of their stubborn leaders.

Now, as he was hungry, he looked for fruit on a fig tree. Finding no fruit upon it but only leaves, he immediately caused it to wither with his word of authority. That was a symbolic action, by means of which he wanted to teach his disciples a profound lesson. The cursed fig tree was a picture of the terrible fate that would befall his people, the city of Jerusalem, which had been planted in God's garden. Since this people, in spite of God's kindness and patience, and in spite of outward religious services and sacrifices, still did not bring forth the fruits of repentance and of faith, it had to fall under judgment.

In the same way today the Lord will not be satisfied with the mere leafy decoration of Christian forms, beautiful services, pious words and feelings. He desires above all the good fruits of a spiritual life: repentance and faith, loving obedience to God in action and in suffering, self-denying love to our neighbor, and conscientious faithfulness in our earthly and heavenly calling. But where do we find these fruits? How many Christian churches have already fallen under the same curse of withering because they lacked these fruits! In how many countries and communities are there warning signs of God's judgment because at the time of their visitation they did not consider what served their peace!

But to those who feel struck by God's judgment, who do not complain of their enemies or their fate but lament over their own sins and faithfully hold out in living trust in God – to such, God the Lord gives a comforting promise. In his strength they too shall do what he did to the fig tree. By holding firmly together in faith and prayer, they shall succeed in making the enemy's powers that oppose God wither and die away, so that they are no longer able to harm the Lord's little flock. Yes, in the power of faith the faithful shall move mountains – the mountains of their worries and needs but most of all the mountains of sin – and cast them into the sea of grace. Whoever holds firmly and faithfully to the promise and is loyal in the discipleship of Christ will experience the fulfillment of this promise.

17

Thursday Morning

Where Is the Room?

Then came the day of Unleavened Bread, on which the Pass-over lamb had to be sacrificed. So Jesus sent Peter and John, saying, "Go and prepare the Passover for us, that we may eat it." They said to him, "Where will you have us prepare it?" He said to them, "Behold, when you have entered the city, a man carrying a jar of water will meet you. Follow him into the house that he enters and tell the master of the house, 'The Teacher says to you, Where is the guest room, where I may eat the Passover with my disciples?' And he will show you a large upper room furnished; prepare it there." And they went and found it just as he had told them, and they prepared the Passover.

Luke 22:7–13

THE STORY of the Lord's suffering leads us into the depths of unfathomable pain, but it also offers us much comfort. One such comforting event is the story of the preparation of the Passover. Even as we feel the painful poverty of the Son of Man who had no home of his own in which to celebrate with his disciples, we are touched by the courageous obedience and faith of the disciples whom the Lord sent out. They sensed the danger threatening the Master and them too in Jerusalem. They had no idea where and how they were to meet the unknown man with the jar of water in the city crowded with pilgrims to the festival. Nevertheless they went without protest, trusting the Lord's instructions.

Here Jesus once more lets rays of his wondrous farseeing vision shine out into the darkness of his way of suffering in order to strengthen the faith of his disciples. The disciples soon find the man whom he indicated, a secret follower of the Lord. He is carrying home a jar that he has just filled with water – but now his heart's longing is to be filled with the water of life.

At the words, "The Teacher says to you," his soul thrills with joy. For the one Master whom he honored, as the other disciples did, has recognized his longing and wants to come to his house. "Where is the guest room where I may eat the Passover with my disciples?" The unknown man immediately understands this question. He does not give the apostles information as to where they might find a suitable room elsewhere, but with joyful readiness he opens his own house to them, giving them the use of his large room, carpeted and furnished with cushions.

As dismaying as the fact is that "he came to his own, and his own people did not receive him," the words that follow are encouraging: "But to all who did receive him, he gave the right to become children of God" (John 1:11–12). There were some among his own people who received him in faith, and one of them was this householder.

At this time of Lent the Lord turns to us too and asks our hearts the question, "Where is the room?" And he says, "Behold, I stand at the door and knock. If anyone hears my voice and opens the door, I will come in to him and eat with him, and he with me" (Rev. 3:20). What a guest! What grace to be allowed to keep the Passover with him, to celebrate the Lord's Supper with him! It is a wonderful task to prepare a guest room for him; still more wonderful is the joy of welcoming him. But the glory of being with him in eternity is a joy beyond our conceiving.

18

Thursday Evening

The Passover Meal

Now before the Feast of the Passover, when Jesus knew that his hour had come to depart out of this world to the Father, having loved his own who were in the world, he loved them to the end.

And when the hour came, he reclined at table, and the apostles with him. And he said to them, "I have earnestly desired to eat this Passover with you before I suffer. For I tell you I will not eat it until it is fulfilled in the kingdom of God." And he took a cup, and when he had given thanks he said, "Take this, and divide it among yourselves. For I tell you that from now on I will not drink of the fruit of the vine until the kingdom of God comes."

John 13:1; Luke 22:14–18

ON THE THURSDAY EVENING before Easter, the Lord and his disciples entered the room that was prepared for the festival and sat down. He knew that this was the last Passover that he would celebrate with his disciples on earth, and they too were filled with anxious fears. Then the Lord opened his mouth and said, "I have earnestly desired to eat this Passover with you before I suffer." What was the reason for this earnest longing? He knew how decisive this meal was for him. He knew that arrest, torture, and death would follow. But the power of love overcame all fear. "Having loved his own, he loved them to the end." He wanted once more to share a peaceful meal with his faithful disciples, who had left everything to follow him. He wanted to lay his last teachings on their hearts and impart heavenly comfort to their souls, to give them strength to endure even the most difficult things for his sake. He longed once more to be refreshed and comforted by their fellowship of love. But his vision saw beyond this.

The Passover was a festival in memory of Israel's liberation from slavery in Egypt, but at the same time it was a prophecy of the freeing of the whole of humankind from the heavy yoke of sin and condemnation through the atoning death of the perfect Paschal Lamb. It was his earnest longing now to fulfill this 1500-year-old prophecy and at long last to redeem the lost world through his sacrificial death, to close in this way the old covenant and set up the new one. But he saw still further beyond this deed of redemption. He looked into that sunny distance beyond time where his whole work would be brought to perfection, where he would celebrate the meal of joy on the transfigured earth with a redeemed humankind and drink with them the new fruit of the vine.

The Lord's earnest longing is the same for all Christians throughout all ages and in all nations and for us too. But alas, how dull are our hearts, how lukewarm is our love for him, how little do we understand what he feels and does for us! Certainly in our hearts is also an abyss of longing and yearning, but all too often our wishes and desires are set only upon transient earthly pleasures, which can never satisfy us and bring us true happiness. We draw water from broken cisterns, and if we continue in this futile way we are bound to languish miserably with our thirst unquenched. Oh, that we might learn to bring all our thoughts into one high longing and endeavor: that we might set them completely on him who has loved us so ardently, and in whom alone we find peace!

The Disciples Quarrel

A dispute also arose among them, as to which of them was to be regarded as the greatest. And he said to them, "The kings of the Gentiles exercise lordship over them, and those in authority over them are called benefactors. But not so with you. Rather, let the greatest among you become as the youngest, and the leader as one who serves. For who is the greater, one who reclines at table or one who serves? Is it not the one who reclines at table? But I am among you as the one who serves. You are those who have stayed with me in my trials, and I assign to you, as my Father assigned to me, a kingdom, that you may eat and drink at my table in my kingdom and sit on thrones judging the twelve tribes of Israel."

Luke 22:24–30

THE WEAKNESSES and mistakes of his own disciples were among the heaviest burdens that the Lord had to bear, even during his farewell meal. While he was expressing the longing of his heart all should have been filled with heavenly peace, yet a quarrel arose among the disciples as to which of them was the greatest. So the Lord now had to reprove their pride. He did this by pointing out that it is a characteristic of the worldly mind to strive to be great. Pride, ambition, and the lust for power are here exposed as the motive of world history. How many thriving countrysides have been laid waste, how much blood, how many tears have been shed simply because the mighty of the earth want to rule! Similar sins are to be found in smaller circles and in many families as well. Children rise up against their parents, subjects against their superiors – because each wants to be lord himself. Christ, on the other hand, emphasizes that to serve in humility is an essential principle of his kingdom. The Lord himself, for whom all the crowns of this world are too paltry, whom the angels of heaven worship, became the servant of all. His whole life on earth was continual serving.

He obeyed his parents; he helped the most wretched of the poor; he washed the feet of his disciples; he bore the heaviest and most infamous of all burdens, the curse of our sin, in inconceivable degradation. And we, pitiable human beings, want to give ourselves airs and in beggarly pride place ourselves above others! We do not become small and humble until under Christ's burden (that is, under the heavy load of our own sin and guilt and under the wonderful load of his compassion) the heart of our old nature is broken. When we become humble the Lord will become our highest and loveliest, our all in all. Only then can a beam of the comfort that he gave his ashamed disciples rise upon us too. He accepted the faithfulness that they had shown him, such as it was, and looking ahead regarded it as perfected and assured them that they would have full share in the kingdom of his future glory.

The time they spent with him was also a school of humility, a daily lesson in becoming smaller. We too must go through the true school of humility in the discipleship of Christ; then our whole life and work become self-sacrificing service. Blessed is the Christian who bears others, even the most unworthy of them, in love for his Savior's sake! Blessed is the king who in all his ruling strives only to serve his people! In view of the glory that the Lord promises his faithful followers, it must become clear to us that it is contemptuous folly to risk eternal happiness for the passing honors of this world. In the final, perfect kingdom the most humble one will be the first – Christ, the eternal king. All the redeemed will be close to him, but those who resembled him most in humility will be closest of all. Free from all envy, each will rejoice at the honoring of the others, and all will know that it is only out of grace that they wear the crown of life.

20

Friday Evening

Foot Washing as Symbol

He rose from supper. He laid aside his outer garments, and taking a towel, tied it around his waist. Then he poured water into a basin and began to wash the disciples' feet and to wipe them with the towel that was wrapped around him. He came to Simon Peter, who said to him, "Lord, do you wash my feet?" Jesus answered him, "What I am doing you do not understand now, but afterward you will understand." Peter said to him, "You shall never wash my feet." Jesus answered him, "If I do not wash you, you have no share with me." Simon Peter said to him, "Lord, not my feet only but also my hands and my head!" Jesus said to him, "The one who has bathed does not need to wash, except for his feet, but is completely clean. And you are clean, but not every one of you."

John 13:4–10

"I AM AMONG YOU as one who serves," the Lord had just said (Luke 22:27). Now he arose and gave proof of this word in deed by washing the feet of all those sitting at table, a service that had been neglected. The Lord of glory, who knew that the Father had given everything into his hands, knelt down in front of his sinful disciples and washed their dusty feet. This moving act is symbolic of his spiritual work of love upon his disciples.

Judas is cold and silent as he allows this menial service to be done to him. The other disciples are amazed and ashamed yet submit to what their Lord is doing. When, however, he approaches Peter with the basin, the disciple draws his feet away in alarm and cries out, "Lord, do you wash my feet?" Here once more the impulsive disciple gives such lovable expression to natural feeling! Nothing can humble him more deeply than such a service done by the Master. But this bitter humiliation is a wholesome medicine that the Lord cannot spare his Peter. He seeks to calm his resistance with friendly words of encouragement, "What I am doing you do not understand now, but afterward you will understand." But Peter cannot be quiet and cries more vehemently, "Never!" Then the Lord overcomes his resistance with the severe words, "If I do not wash you, you have no share in me." No share in him? Peter cannot bear that.

Where could he go if he were to have no share in him who is his life, his all? He is completely disarmed and softened. He also begins to sense the significance of the washing, and in a flood of emotion he calls out, "Lord, not my feet only but also my hands and my head!" But here he has misfired again. At this time the Lord wants only to wash his feet. For whoever has had a bath – as was the custom before the festival – needs only to have his dusty feet washed in order to be clean.

Through their community with the Lord the disciples were purified and sanctified as by a holy bath. But he wanted to cleanse them of the daily stains through his forgiving work of love. He does the same thing to all his own through the ages. The bath is like baptism, which unites us with Christ and makes us God's beloved children. The washing of the feet points to the constantly renewed forgiveness of the sins that cling to us – such as we experience after every repentant prayer and in each celebration of the Lord's Supper shared in faith. But the Lord also works for our betterment through the humiliations and suffering in our lives. Those who continually pray for forgiveness with repentant hearts will find peace in the blessed truth: "The blood of Jesus Christ, the Son of God, cleanses us from all sin" (1 John 1:7). Whether they are aware of it or not, they will receive the heavenly powers of sanctification and so be prepared to belong one day to the throngs around the throne who have washed their robes in the blood of the Lamb (Rev. 7:14).

21

Saturday Morning

Foot Washing as Example

When he had washed their feet and put on his outer garments and resumed his place, he said to them, "Do you understand what I have done to you? You call me Teacher and Lord, and you are right, for so I am. If I then, your Lord and Teacher, have washed your feet, you also ought to wash one another's feet. For I have given you an example, that you also should do just as I have done to you. Truly, truly, I say to you, a servant is not greater than his master, nor is a messenger greater than the one who sent him. If you know these things, blessed are you if you do them.

John 13:12–17

"**DO YOU UNDERSTAND** what I have done to you?" the Lord asked his disciples after washing their feet. He asks us the same thing every time we have been helped through humiliation and distress. He asks it especially, however, in the time of Lent, and every time we celebrate the Lord's Supper or hear the message of salvation. In all these things he is carrying on the loving service of washing our feet and working for our sanctification.

But he is also giving us an example, that we should wash one another's feet by serving in love. We know all this, but knowledge alone is of no use to us. For the Lord adds, "If you know these things, blessed are you if you do them." Here the Lord uncovers the deepest source of our wretchedness and lack of inward peace. It is the gaping cleft between what we know and what we do. We know God's will, but we do not act on it. The more clearly we know it without doing it, the greater will be our condemnation. So our old heart has to break in repentant sorrow and we need to receive a new heart through our Savior's work of love. The Spirit of Christ must fill and pervade us to enable us to follow his example and bring what we do into harmony with what we know.

It is the noble task of every Christian to serve his neighbor untiringly in love. There is no lack of opportunity for this: nursing sick parents or children with love and patience and, if necessary, literally washing their feet; helping a family in distress; providing clothes for someone who is very cold, or a place of refuge for a lost child. In every case, however, the main thing is to wash the feet of our neighbor spiritually, that is to say, to cleanse their soul from the stains of sin by leading them to the purifying bath of Christ's compassionate love. As Christ's disciples, we have to bear the mistakes and shortcomings of others and forgive again and again all that hurts and offends us. "Love bears all things, believes all things, hopes all things, endures all things" (1 Cor. 13:7).

At the same time of course, following Christ's example, we must not hold back sharp-edged truth and serious admonition, for our aim is to set the other's better self free from the yoke of sin. Gold is purified only by the heat of the fire. It would be truly uncompassionate to let our neighbor go to spiritual ruin through consideration for the flesh. But we can do such a work of love in the right spirit only if we lay the erring brother upon the Savior's heart in prayer, only if we constantly think of his true happiness and in humble love give him a good example ourselves. In doing this we shall soon experience that our own hearts will find comfort, as the Lord says, "If you know these things, blessed are you if you do them."

22

Saturday Evening

One of You
Is Going to Betray Me

After saying these things, Jesus was troubled in his spirit, and testified, "Truly, truly, I say to you, one of you will betray me." The disciples looked at one another, uncertain of whom he spoke.

And they were very sorrowful and began to say to him one after another, "Is it I, Lord?"

John 13:21–22; Matthew 26:22

AFTER THE LORD had washed his disciples' feet, he was troubled in spirit. For some time already he had looked with sorrow into Judas's heart. Ever since the anointing in Bethany, Judas had been a burden upon him, and here at the farewell meal he felt weighed down by its pressure. The very presence of the lurking traitor in the circle of his closest friends was heavy on his soul. The hand that had already taken the thirty silver pieces dipped into the one bowl with him. But still more deeply did it pain the Lord that this disciple, whose soul he continued to seek, would not be held back from the way of destruction by any power of love. Jesus knew how blessedly joyful even Judas might have become. At the same time he saw the abyss toward which the lost soul was rushing headlong. Because he could not use force, he had to leave this soul to the enemy.

What can compare to the sorrow expressed in the Lord's words: "Truly, truly, I say to you, one of you will betray me"? At the same time these words are a profound expression of the Master's pastoral care for his disciples. Through his cry of pain, all twelve are deeply humbled. Each one feels urgently admonished to examine his own heart. The traitor is treated with consideration in that his name is not mentioned. Once more the merciful Master opens a door for him to turn back. This momentous saying was not without decisive effect. For Judas, to be sure, it became a word of judgment. But the others were dismayed and distressed. They felt struck, and looking into the hidden depths of their hearts, were filled with alarm about themselves. They were convinced that the Lord knew them best, and turning to him they asked in humble sincerity, "Is it I, Lord?" This question contained the hope that it was not them and that the Lord would be able to reassure them.

Is it I? We also will have to ask that frightened question when the gospel's call to repentance places before our eyes all who have deserted, denied, and betrayed the Lord, persecuted him, and brought him to the cross. When the story of Christ's passion reminds us of those dark deeds, we should not look at others but feel struck ourselves to see the roots of those sins in our own hearts. We should recognize what we would have become if the Lord's grace had not protected us. Moreover, we ought to see with pain that it is we who with our sins have caused the Lord's death agony. He had to suffer and atone for our sins against God, against our neighbor, and against ourselves. Nevertheless, we must not give way to despair but rather confess with childlike hearts: "What thou, my Lord, hast suffered was all for sinners' gain. Mine, mine was the transgression, but thine the deadly pain." Then everything will be reversed by him. He will change the cause of our grief into the cause of our comfort. He will make us certain of this: Yes, it is you who have brought me suffering and death. But it is also you who, in me and with me, are judged, sentenced, and have died, so that in me you have atoned for all that of which you were ever guilty. Be comforted, what is yours is mine and what is mine is yours. Go in peace.

Second Week of Lent

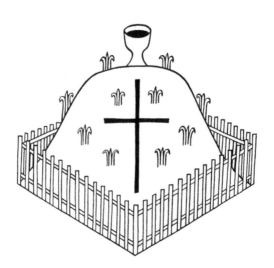

23

Sunday Morning

Judas's Night

He answered, "The Son of Man goes as it is written of him, but woe to that man by whom the Son of Man is betrayed! It would have been better for that man if he had not been born." Judas, who would betray him, answered, "Is it I, Rabbi?" He said to him, "You have said so."

One of his disciples, whom Jesus loved, was reclining at table at Jesus' side, so Simon Peter motioned to him to ask Jesus of whom he was speaking. So that disciple, leaning back against Jesus, said to him, "Lord, who is it?" Jesus answered, "It is he to whom I will give this morsel of bread when I have dipped it." So when he had dipped the morsel, he gave it to Judas, the son of Simon Iscariot. Then after he had taken the morsel, Satan entered into him. Jesus said to him, "What you are going to do, do quickly." Now no one at the table knew why he said this to him. Some thought that, because Judas had the moneybag, Jesus was telling him, "Buy what we need for the feast," or that he should give something to the poor. So, after receiving the morsel of bread, he immediately went out. And it was night.

Matthew 26:24–25; John 13:23–30

JUST AS THE ORIGIN OF EVIL is an unfathomable mystery, so the figure of Judas appears to us as a dark enigma. We will never find an answer to the questions, "Why was he chosen as an apostle, since his end was not hidden from the All-Knowing One? What is the relation between necessity and freedom in what he did?" This much, however, is clear to us: even the blackest crimes have to serve in carrying out the Almighty's plans for his kingdom, and yet the criminals themselves must bear responsibility. Furthermore, even enlightened disciples can become traitors. Then, the higher they stand the deeper their fall. Finally, there is nothing so disastrous for believing Christians as wanting to serve two masters, that is, to foster sin while following Christ. Judas's love of self and love of the world was a special attachment to money. His heart was hardened through greed, and greed made him a thief.

His awareness that the Lord saw through him made it more and more difficult for Judas to remain with Jesus. But at the same time, as long as he hoped that

Jesus was the Messiah, he felt compelled to hide behind the iron mask of hypocrisy. His devotion changed to enmity, and when he finally saw that the Galilean's cause was hopeless, he betrayed him. This Master was to perish, and the traitor wanted a place in the ruling party for himself. Thus he sat at the meal and heard the Lord's cry of sorrow: "One of you will betray me!" It flashed like lightning through his soul. It may be that his conscience stirred once more, but he struck it down. So he also asked, with total hypocrisy, "Is it I, Rabbi?" And the Lord answered, "You have said so." Then the devil entered into him. His will became one with Satan's will. He himself became one heart and one soul with the prince of darkness. Now the Lord had to give him up, and he pressed him to go out: "What you are going to do, do quickly." That was all right with Judas; he could hardly endure this company any longer. And now speed was necessary if the hellish deed was to succeed. He left the room quickly and hurried to the high priests. "And it was night" – night outside, and deeper night in his soul, eternal night.

In shining contrast to Judas at the Last Supper, we see the figure of John. He was lying close to the breast of Jesus. He was "the disciple whom the Lord loved." Jesus loved all his disciples, but John was more open to his love than the others. In his surrender he resembled Mary and in nature he was the one most like the Master. In fellowship with Jesus the spirit of the son of thunder had been transfigured into the spirit of holy love. He could never forget that he was "the disciple whom the Lord loved" and who had lain close to his breast. That remained the joy of his life, as his whole Gospel testifies.

Whoever would come as close to the Lord as John did should immerse himself in the Gospel of this disciple until that face full of grace and truth appears to him and fills his being with joy.

24

Sunday Evening

The Appointment of the Holy Supper

The Lord Jesus on the night when he was betrayed took bread, and when he had given thanks, he broke it, and said, "This is my body which is for you. Do this in remembrance of me." In the same way also he took the cup, after supper, saying, "This cup is the new covenant in my blood. Do this, as often as you drink it, in remembrance of me."

1 Cor. 11:23–25

IF WE IN SPIRIT enter the room where the farewell meal is being held, we feel surrounded by the air of heaven and by the peace of God. After the departure of the traitor the Lord breathed more freely, and he appointed the meal of the new covenant – a fulfillment of the promise given in the Passover and a prophecy of the eternal, heavenly meal of joy. Raising his eyes, he gave thanks; blessing the bread, he broke it, then handed it to his disciples. He also took the cup and gave it to them saying, "Take, eat – take, drink!"

Those words are a testament, for they are the words of one taking leave, the words of the Redeemer who is about to die. In this word "Take!" the Lord lays all his love, all his work of redemption. With it he commits to his disciples all that he has done for them and all that he will still fulfill through his suffering and death. Throughout all centuries since then he speaks to his church at celebrations of the Lord's Supper: "Take!" Every time we hear it we should remember that we have nothing to bring to the Lord to earn his salvation. On the contrary, our whole life as Christians ought to be a daily taking, thankfully drawing out of the well of his grace.

The special gift of grace that the Lord offers his own, when he says, "Eat, drink!" is at once physical and spiritual: the physical gifts of the bread and wine are also symbols of the spiritual gift of grace, the invisible heavenly food. The Lord indicates this with the mysterious saying, "This is my body – this is my blood." He gives his disciples not only the blessed fruit of his suffering, death, and resurrection, but also his very self, his most holy person. Thus he celebrates in the Holy Supper his entrance into the hearts of those who believe in him. His powers flow through them, his life becomes their life. Nor is their frail earthly body rejected. It is fed with the food of heaven in order that it may have part one day in the great resurrection of complete transfiguration in the heavenly meal.

This sacrament is a communion, that is, a meal of community. It is first a mysterious community of the bread and wine with the body and blood of the Lord in accordance with the words, "The cup of blessing that we bless, is it not a participation in the blood of Christ? The bread that we break, is it not a participation in the body of Christ?" (1 Cor. 10:16). Further, the Lord brings about such deep and intimate community of life with his disciples that it exceeds all asking and understanding. It enables them to say, "It is no longer I who live, but Christ who lives in me" (Gal. 2:20).

Finally, the members of the Lord's Supper of all times are bound in a living unity which scripture calls the body of Christ. All who throng to the Lord's table – the weary and heavy laden, longing for help and seeking forgiveness and comfort, strength, and peace – can see with spiritual eyes their glorified Lord at the meal of grace. They can open their hearts to him who has given us the great promise, "Behold, I stand at the door and knock. If anyone hears my voice and opens the door, I will come in to him and eat with him, and he with me" (Rev. 3:20).

25

Monday Morning

For the Forgiveness of Sins

"This is my body, which is given for you."

"This is my blood of the new covenant, which is poured out for you and for many for the forgiveness of sins."

Luke 22:19; Matthew 26:28

FORGIVENESS OF SINS – that is what we need. Sin is the greatest evil, so our most urgent need is for forgiveness. We cannot forgive our own sins. We cannot quiet our conscience by means of diversion, work, or sleep. It awakes again and again, embittering all our joy and making us afraid of death. We need forgiveness every day – when we get up and when we go to bed. We need it when the sins of our children remind us of our own, or when we stand by our parents' graves. We need forgiveness in youth and in age, and we need it in the hour of judgment. Our faithful Savior knows better than we that without forgiveness we would sink into eternal night. That is why he came to seek and to save the lost. That is why he submitted to bear our punishment – the cruel flogging and the excruciating crucifixion. And as he died he even prayed, "Father, forgive them" (Luke 23:34).

In order to gain our forgiveness, he let his body be broken in death and his blood be spilled on the accursed tree. Now he can bend down to us and say, "Given for you, poured out for you, for the forgiveness of sins." This "for you" is a blessed word. It is the key to the kingdom of heaven, and with it we may dare draw near to the just God. Through this word our life is made holy and our death is overcome.

But this word "for you" requires believing hearts. It must be made our own in prayer and striving. We must first become quite poor and small and empty of all delusion as to our own worth. We must have nothing left to us but to cry for God's mercy. Then the Lord reveals himself to us in his passion. He lets us see him in the agony of his death, in the lamentation of his cry, "My God, my God, why have you forsaken me?" (Matt. 27:46) – and he bends down to us with the promise "for you!" Every Christian should lay hold of this word with all his strength, and have it mean "for me."

How precious it is, when we have dragged ourselves along and have lost heart under the weight of our sins, to receive the certainty in the Holy Supper: You are forgiven. Everything, everything has been forgiven forever! Then we can weep for our sins, but these will be blessed tears. For where there is forgiveness of sins there is also life and joy.

Forgiveness of sins, life, and joy are the three gifts of heaven, which nowhere on earth are offered to us in such full measure as at the Lord's table. Those for whom such a table has been spread can go through this vale of tears and yet sing with the psalmist, "The Lord is my shepherd, I shall not want" (Ps. 23:1). They walk their pilgrimage as poor and yet rich, as sorrowful yet always rejoicing, as having nothing and yet possessing everything (2 Cor. 6:10) – until one day they shall experience to the full: "Blessed are those who are invited to the marriage supper of the Lamb" (Rev. 19:9).

26

Monday Evening

Do This in Remembrance of Me

And when he had given thanks, he broke it, and said, "This is my body which is for you. Do this in remembrance of me."

1 Cor. 11:24

THE LORD'S SUPPER is not only a meal of community and of reconciliation but also a meal of remembrance, for the Lord himself said when he appointed it, "Do this in remembrance of me." With the word "Do this" he gives his church the command and the authority to celebrate again and again throughout all time the meal which he appointed. In doing this he looks into the distant future. He sees great throngs of sinners in need of redemption drawing near, millions of Christians out of every nation eating and drinking and, at his table, receiving forgiveness, life, and joy.

In adding, "in remembrance of me," he shows that he intends the Holy Supper to be a celebration that reminds us of the redemption of the world from sin, death, and the devil, accomplished by his death. The word "remember" comes from the Latin root meaning "call to mind, be mindful"; so it is a sin to come thoughtlessly to this celebration and keep it as a purely outward ceremony.

We should turn our whole mind and spirit to the Lord, to his reconciling death, and to what he has brought about through it. But to remember also means to contemplate, to see before us in spirit – that is, we should share inwardly what the disciples experienced at that time, and what the Lord did, said, and suffered. We should place ourselves at that first Lord's Supper and in spirit experience how the Lord gave his disciples his testament, how he broke down in Gethsemane, how he was torn by lashes in the judgment hall, and crowned with thorns. Then we should see him on the cross, his blood flowing for us from deeply struck wounds and his body broken for us. We should see him languishing there until all was accomplished and he could commend his spirit into his Father's hands.

"Remembering," in its deepest sense, can mean to feel his presence. The Lord is present in person at the Holy Supper, wanting to meet and bless us. In adoration we experience that the holy person of the Crucified and Risen One is at work in the midst of his church when it unites to celebrate the Lord's Supper.

When we add to this the words of the apostle Paul: "As often as you eat this bread and drink the cup, you proclaim the Lord's death until he comes" (1 Cor. 11:26), we realize that the Lord has set up in the Lord's Supper an imperishable monument to himself and to his death. It will remain when all monuments of stone and bronze have crumbled. This celebration should be, in fact, a proclamation that never grows silent, addressed to his disciples and his whole church. Yes, it should continue to be a mighty testimony to the victorious power of Christ's death to the whole world, until he himself will come again in majesty to establish the kingdom of his glory. As for us, as we prepare to keep the Lord's Supper in order to proclaim his death, we should deliver up our old nature to death and present our whole life as a sacrifice of love and gratitude to the Lord.

27

Tuesday Morning

The New Commandment

"Little children, yet a little while I am with you. You will seek me, and just as I said to the Jews, so now I also say to you, 'Where I am going you cannot come.' A new commandment I give to you, that you love one another: just as I have loved you, you also are to love one another. By this all people will know that you are my disciples, if you have love for one another."

John 13:33–35

THE HOLY SUPPER is also a love meal. As the hour of farewell for the Lord and his disciples drew nearer, the Master got ready to go to death for his own, and his love welled up richly from its source in his heart. Although his was not a weak and sentimental love, he could not exhaust himself in expressions of the deepest tenderness. He washed his disciples' feet. He described them as his friends. He even called the men, browned by wind and weather, "little children" in the overflowing love of a mother. He did everything he possibly could to comfort them about his death and to strengthen them for the tasks and struggles facing them. Thus he committed his last will to their care by saying, "A new commandment I give you, that you love one another; just as I have loved you, you also are to love one another."

Now, what is new in this commandment? God is eternally love. He has always wanted his children, who were made in his image, to walk in love. He already impressed upon his people of the old covenant that they should love their neighbor (Lev. 19:18; Isa. 58:7). But this commandment did indeed become new when Jesus gave it. It is new because we are to love one another as he has loved us. The example is new, for perfect love is seen only in Christ. Only through him has the meaning of love become clear, namely, self-denial, dedication to loved ones, sacrificing of one's life for them, and indissoluble community with them.

For Christ's disciples the basis of the commandment is also new: the redemption common to them all through his sacrificial death and the community of life given them by his dwelling in them. The extent of love is also new. If until now love was limited to the members of the clan or tribe, it is now to include everyone, all who are suffering and in need and even the worst enemies. From now on, this love is to be the breath of life of his church and the sign by which his disciples are known. This truly took form in the church of the first Christians. They were of one heart and one soul, and with amazement Jews and Gentiles had to cry out, "See how they love one another!"

But can that holy characteristic of the disciples of Christ be seen today? Look into your hearts and families, your churches and countries! Alas! Where is there love? Egotism, covetousness, and self-conceit rule people's minds; envy and dissension ruin the churches. Why are we so discontented and weighed down by care, so far from God, from blessedness and joy? Because we are without love. Oh, how happy we would be if we could really love – love as Christ loved us! But how can we attain this? The Lord himself gives the answer: "Abide in my love"(John 15:9). Only when we immerse ourselves more and more deeply in his love, only when we let ourselves be loved more and more by him – yes, loved out of our selfishness and death – will our hearts become new, warm, and joyful in community of love with all the dearly bought souls whom the Lord leads to us.

28

Tuesday Evening

Peter Is Warned

The Lord said, "Simon, Simon, behold, Satan demanded to have you, that he might sift you like wheat, but I have prayed for you that your faith may not fail. And when you have turned again, strengthen your brothers." Peter said to him, "Lord, I am ready to go with you both to prison and to death."

And to all the disciples Jesus said, "You will all fall away because of me this night; for it is written, 'I will strike the shepherd, and the sheep of the flock will be scattered.' But after I am raised up, I will go before you to Galilee." Peter answered him. "Though they all fall away because of you, I will never fall away." Jesus said to him, "Truly, I tell you, this very night, before the rooster crows, you will deny me three times."

Luke 22:31–33; Matthew 26:31–34

IT WAS ONE OF THE LORD'S most painful experiences that on his way to death he also had to endure the unfaithfulness of his disciples. With deep sadness he told them that the evil hour of temptation was near them, in which Satan would want to sift them like wheat. He told them that they would all fall away because of him that very night, and that a still deeper fall awaited Peter through a three-fold denial. But at the same time he comforted them with the promise that they would meet again soon in Galilee, that Peter would turn around, and most of all with the assurance that his praying for them would protect their faith. The disciples indeed contradicted the reproachful prophecy, but the sifting had to take place in order to purge and purify them.

The yawning abyss opened its depths to swallow them all. What would have become of them if the hand of the faithful Shepherd had not been held over them, protecting them? What would have become of Peter if the enemy of souls had succeeded in filling him with black despair after his denial, as he did Judas? But the mighty intercession of his Master, who was about to die for him, guarded a last spark of faith deep in Peter's heart even in the darkest hour and saw to it that it did not go out. Under the protection of the Lord, the sifting was not allowed to destroy the disciples. On the contrary, it served as wholesome humiliation and inner renewal. In the storm of temptation the chaff of self-confidence was blown away, but the pure wheat of the rebirth brought about by grace remained in the humbled hearts, bringing blessing.

For us, too, hours of sifting must come. We cannot and may not be spared them. Only in the fire of temptation the dross of natural youth and self-conceit is burned away. Only in the furnace of distress and humiliation the gold of faith is refined. But these are painful and anxious experiences. How would we have fared if in times of weakness and doubt, of despondency or passion, the murderer of souls had been permitted to bring all his power against us? Into what an abyss would we sink if in the hour of death and of judgment an almighty, faithful hand would not cover and hold us? But the promise of the compassionate High Priest also holds good for each one of us. His prayer has carried us too. It has prevented our falling away from him until now, and it will continue to shield and help us in the hour of our greatest fear. This prayer will bring it about that finally the last chaff is winnowed from our lives and we, as pure wheat, are gathered into the garner of eternal love.

29

Wednesday Morning

I Am Going to the Father

"A little while, and you will see me no longer; and again a little while, and you will see me."

John 16:16

AFTER THE APPOINTMENT of the Lord's Supper, Jesus spoke such words as never came from human lips. They were full of the sadness of farewell, of majesty, and of peace. After he had promised to send them the Holy Spirit and with comforting words prepared them for what they would suffer, he said about his own death, "A little while, and you will see me no longer!" In this way he told them that his death was very near and the night of the grave would soon hide him from their sight. But when he added, "Again a little while, and you will see me," he was seeing beyond death and the grave. He was promising that he would rise again soon and comforting both himself and his own with the approach of Easter, when they would have him again.

Yet in these words there lie further prophetic aspects, for through his ascension his visible presence was to be withdrawn again from the eyes of his disciples, both then and in the future. Yet, once again in a little while, that is to say when their life was completed, they would be united again with him in his Father's kingdom. The whole world epoch from the time of his ascension until his return is compressed here in the vision of the Son of God into "a little while." When he appears in his glory, the blessed meal of the eternities will begin, and no power can any longer disturb his perfect community with his disciples.

Linked to this revelation of his goal are the words: "I go to the Father"(John 16:10). From the shining heights of heaven he came from the Father down to this poor earth. Now he wanted to return to the Father. The whole of his life as Savior was simply "going to the Father." Already as a boy he had sought and found his Father in the temple. His prayers and thanksgiving had constantly led him to the heart of the Father. His deeds, struggles, and suffering were accomplished in the Father's name and for his honor, and all his striving was set toward the return to his Father's house. So even the way to death had now to be transfigured into a way to the Father.

Christ's way should also become our way. What wondrous light will brighten our otherwise dark pilgrimage when our life becomes a way to the Father. We should draw near to him daily with trust and love, with gratitude and prayer. Even when we have gone astray and made bad mistakes, we should not seek refuge and help from the world but return through the entry prepared by Christ. Like the prodigal son we should return repentant into the arms of the Father that are also open for us. Then our actions, thoughts, and desires will gain a firm direction. When we accompany our parents or children to the grave, it will comfort us that they have gone home to the Father's house, and after a little while we will see them again. When the last hour comes for ourselves, we will overcome the fear and horror of death with the confident faith that "I am going to the Father."

30

Wednesday Evening

The High Priestly Prayer

When Jesus had spoken these words, he lifted up his eyes to heaven, and said, "Father, the hour has come; glorify your Son that the Son may glorify you, since you have given him authority over all flesh, to give eternal life to all whom you have given him. And this is eternal life, that they know you the only true God, and Jesus Christ whom you have sent. I glorified you on earth, having accomplished the work that you gave me to do. And now, Father, glorify me in your own presence with the glory that I had with you before the world existed."

John 17:1–5

AFTER THE LORD had ended the farewell celebration with the song of praise, he and his disciples arose from the meal, and standing in their midst he prayed that unique prayer which we call the High Priestly Prayer. The words are clear and simple, but the content opens to us immeasurable depths of divine truth and eternal life, before which our limited mind and spirit stand still in reverence.

The first part of this prayer contains our High Priest's plea for his own glorification. He lifted up his eyes to heaven and said, "Father, the hour has come; glorify your Son." He had reached the end of his course on earth. He had completed his great, saving work and had accomplished all that his Father had sent him to do. With a peace and joy such as no one else feels in the face of death, he could testify to the Father, "I glorified you on earth, having accomplished the work that you gave me to do."

Just a few (though very terrible) hours of the agony of death still lay before him. But he was determined to hold out and in anticipation spoke of them here as already accomplished: "And now, Father, glorify me in your own presence with the glory that I had with you before the world existed." With this he opens to his own a glimpse into the mysteries of heaven, things into which angels long to look (1 Pet. 1:12), which God has revealed to those who love him. We are led here into the eternal fellowship of love of the Father and the Son, into the Father's heart and into his gracious decree for the redemption of the world. We are led into the

Son's heart and into his inexpressible longing for his heavenly glorification. Indeed, the High Priest reveals to us the depths of this longing when he says, "That the Son may glorify you." His soul thirsted for the Father to be glorified in the crown of his creation, man. But it was necessary first for the Son himself to be glorified and lifted up to the Father's right hand and for the Holy Spirit to be poured out, in order to bring salvation to lost sinners and eternal life to the children of death. And ever since the first Pentecost he has carried on his gracious work on this otherwise poor earth through the Holy Spirit. For eternal life is not merely a matter of the future beyond death, but is already given here on earth into the hearts of those who come to the Father through the Son and become God's children. That is made known to us by the Lord's wonderful, deep words: "And this is eternal life, that they know you the only true God, and Jesus Christ whom you have sent."

Even as the eternal divinity of the Son shines overpoweringly in this part of Christ's prayer, we are comforted to perceive also an outstanding characteristic of his human nature: longing. By nature we are all children of longing. Nothing is planted so deeply in our breast as longing. Much in us can die: hope can fade, love grow cold, perception become dull. But longing remains. It fills the breast of youth, it goes hand in hand with the melancholy of age. Yet it often leads us astray and deludes us with false goals.

But here the Lord Jesus lets us see the true goal of all human longing. For us too it is the transfiguration of our whole being and nature. This takes place when God is glorified in us and through us. He is glorified in us when we acknowledge him as our Father, and he becomes our heart's highest good. He is glorified through us when our whole way of life honors him. Already in the Sermon on the Mount Christ exhorts us, "Let your light shine before others, so that they may see your good works and give glory to your Father who is in heaven" (Matt. 5:16). Transfiguration like this begins here on earth but is completed only in the kingdom of glory above.

31

Thursday Morning

Christ's Prayer for His Apostles

"I have manifested your name to the people whom you gave me out of the world. Yours they were, and you gave them to me, and they have kept your word. Now they know that everything that you have given me is from you. For I have given them the words that you gave me, and they have received them and have come to know in truth that I came from you; and they have believed that you sent me. I am praying for them. I am not praying for the world but for those whom you have given me, for they are yours. All mine are yours, and yours are mine, and I am glorified in them. And I am no longer in the world, but they are in the world, and I am coming to you. Holy Father, keep them in your name, which you have given me, that they may be one, even as we are one. While I was with them, I kept them in your name, which you have given me. I have guarded them, and not one of them has been lost except the son of destruction, that the Scripture might be fulfilled. But now I am coming to you, and these things I speak in the world, that they may

have my joy fulfilled in themselves. I have given them your word, and the world has hated them because they are not of the world, just as I am not of the world. I do not ask that you take them out of the world, but that you keep them from the evil one. They are not of the world, just as I am not of the world. Sanctify them in the truth; your word is truth. As you sent me into the world, so I have sent them into the world. And for their sake I consecrate myself, that they also may be sanctified in truth."

John 17:6–19

AFTER LOOKING UP TO HEAVEN, the eyes of the High Priest were turned to his disciples gathered around him. Just as deeply as he longed for his own transfiguration, he felt the pain of the thought that they were now to be left without him. So he prayed for them, committing them to the Father's care. Like all that he said and did that evening, this prayer was permeated with the most tender love. He could not overemphasize that they were his own, and without a thought of their weaknesses and mistakes, he gave them the good testimony in the presence of the Father that they had kept his word and truly believed in him. But with deep concern he said, "I am coming to you. I am no longer in the world, but they are in the world."

He knew exactly what "being in the world" means. He had experienced it through the opposition of darkness, persecuted by his enemies and Satan's fury. Now his poor, weak disciples were to be exposed to the same storms. While he was with them, he had led and taught them, carried them and blessed them. He had given them his truth, his peace, his spirit. As a hen gathers her brood under her wings he had guarded them, and with one exception, had protected and kept them as his precious possession. Now he had to go away from them. He had to leave them alone – yes, even send them out into this wild, hostile world to continue his work. So with all fervor he commended them in prayer to the loving care of the almighty Father. He could not ask God to take them out of this world. They could not evade their great apostolic task by fleeing from the world, taking shelter in peaceful solitude; on the contrary, they were to work and suffer in the midst of the world in order to glorify their Master, to battle with the world in order to overcome it. Thus their Savior does not ask his Father to take them out of the world, but to protect them in the world. No evil, no power of darkness, no enemy of souls is permitted to corrupt them or destroy their activity. But for their own blessedness and for the carrying out of their mission, the

Lord makes two great petitions: "Keep them in your name," and, "Sanctify them in your truth."

Although we may not have apostolic callings, nevertheless we too have something to learn from this. In the first place, that we have been placed in this world of sin, temptation, and need not in order to flee from it but to overcome it. And in our calling, however insignificant, we must work as though placed there by the Lord. We can only carry this out in a way that is pleasing to God if we are kept in faith and sanctified in the truth.

32

Christ's Prayer
for His Whole Church

"I do not ask for these only, but also for those who will believe in me through their word, that they may all be one, just as you, Father, are in me, and I in you, that they also may be in us, so that the world may believe that you have sent me. The glory that you have given me I have given to them, that they may be one even as we are one, I in them and you in me, that they may become perfectly one, so that the world may know that you sent me and loved them even as you loved me. Father, I desire that they also, whom you have given me, may be with me where I am, to see my glory that you have given me because you loved me before the foundation of the world. O righteous Father, even though the world does not know you, I know you, and these know that you have sent me. I made known to them your name, and I will continue to make it known, that the love with which you have loved me may be in them, and I in them."

John 17:20–26

IF WE FOLLOW the High Priest's intercession prayerfully, we will be amazed at the wealth of his compassion. For he prays not only for his disciples, but also for all who in future will believe in him through their word. That means that we too are included in this intercession. For the whole of Christianity is founded on the gospel proclaimed by the apostles. The Savior's love embraces his whole church throughout all the centuries, and he entrusts all his own, from the first to the last, to the Father. He prays that they may "be one" amongst themselves. In doing so, he expresses the longing that they all walk in community of faith, in peaceful harmony of conviction, and that brotherly love unite them in one great holy organism.

It is not brilliant speeches, high scholarship, or famous deeds that he looks for in his disciples, but he looks again and again for love. Only love has value in his sight. Though they speak with the tongues of men and of angels, have all faith, and give all their goods to the poor, if they have no love, they are nothing (1 Cor. 13:1–3). In the first church at Pentecost his prayer was fulfilled, but where is such love to be found now? Where is it among believers? Where is that unanimity of heart, that unselfish mind that joyfully gives away even earthly property for one's brothers and sisters? Who bears with true patience the faults of even his closest neighbor? Yes, love has grown cold in many. It has become faint and rare in the church. What is the cause of this desperate loss? It is the secularization of the churches, the apathy of the masses, the self-conceit of the religious denominations, the quarrelsomeness of the theologians. Repentance and humility are lacking, as are sincere conversion to God and deep love to Jesus. Love to one another is born out of the fellowship of love with the Father and the Son.

Now the High Priest continues his prayer for those who really become of one heart with Christ and one another. "Father, I desire that they also, whom you have given me, may be with me where I am, to see my glory." How majestic is this "I desire!" Only the Son whose will is one with the Father's will can speak like this. Where he is, he wants his own to be with him too. How comforting that is! Even on earth they are to be with him, in the worship of the church, as in solitary prayer, in the intimate family circle, and in the celebration of the Holy Supper. On paths of joy as well as on their walk through the dark valley, they say to him in faith, "You are with me." Finally we will also be with him in his Father's kingdom where we may fall into his arms and thank him eternally. Truly, with radiant eyes we will see him and his glory. We ourselves will be raised to this glory. Be still, my soul, and worship!

33

Friday Morning

Entering Gethsemane

When Jesus had spoken these words, he went out with his disciples across the brook Kidron, where there was a garden, which he and his disciples entered. Now Judas, who betrayed him, also knew the place; for Jesus often met there with his disciples.

And he said to his disciples, "Sit here, while I go over there and pray. Pray that you may not enter into temptation."

And taking with him Peter and the two sons of Zebedee, he began to be sorrowful and troubled. Then he said to them, "My soul is very sorrowful, even to death; remain here and watch with me."

John 18:1–2; Luke 22:40; Matthew 26:37–38

AFTER THE FAREWELL MEAL the Lord left the room where the supper had been held and set off with his disciples by the light of the full moon. They went through the deep Kidron Valley to the foot of the Mount of Olives. Here was Gethsemane, whose name means "oil press." It was a shady olive orchard, probably surrounded by a stone wall, perhaps with a simple country house in the background.

He left eight of his disciples at the entrance and took the three witnesses of his transfiguration deeper into the garden with him. There they would also witness his abasement. Until now the Lord had spoken to his disciples with tranquility of soul and comforting kindness, mainly of his work of redemption. His High Priestly Prayer had welled up from his soul like a psalm from the heights of heaven. Those around him might have had the impression that the gates of Paradise were already opening to receive redeemed humanity into fellowship with God. But on entering the garden where he was soon to be taken prisoner, where his suffering was to begin in spirit, his whole demeanor changed.

Until now he had stridden forwards, the hero without equal. The wind and sea, sickness and death had obeyed him. The devil and hell had to flee before him. But now his face was pale and his whole body trembled. He began to lament and to be afraid, and poured out his distress to his three closest apostles: "My soul is very sorrowful, even to death."

The dark hour had now come, in which he was to accomplish his saving work by giving himself up voluntarily to the agony of death. This surrender must have been extremely difficult for him, because his death was something quite different from our death. We are by nature children of death. Here, however, the Prince of Life was to die. The Holy One of God was to take upon himself the guilt of all people and the penalty of all sinners. The only begotten Son himself was to be made sin and a curse (Gal. 3:13) and delivered up to the Father's judgment of wrath. Not only human enemies, but devils and hell were to triumph over him, laughing mockingly. He knows all that. He feels and experiences it in a measure of which no human can have an inkling, and at the same time heaven is closed to him and all consolation extinguished. That is why he would like to lay his head on the breast of his poor disciples. That is why he begs them, "Remain here and watch with me!"

Who can measure the depth of his humiliation and fathom the mystery of love that brought him so low? This much we can grasp, however: his sorrow is our salvation and solace in all the distress of death; and we should worship this love that is beyond all understanding.

34

Friday Evening

The Prayer Battle in Gethsemane

And going a little farther, he fell on the ground and prayed that, if it were possible, the hour might pass from him. And he said, "Abba, Father, all things are possible for you. Remove this cup from me. Yet not what I will, but what you will." And he came and found them sleeping, and he said to Peter, "Simon, are you asleep? Could you not watch one hour?"

Again, for the second time, he went away and prayed, "My Father, if this cannot pass unless I drink it, your will be done." And again he came and found them sleeping, for their eyes were heavy. So, leaving them again, he went away and prayed for the third time, saying the same words again.

And there appeared to him an angel from heaven, strengthening him. And being in agony he prayed more earnestly; and his sweat became like great drops of blood falling down to the ground.

Mark 14:35–37; Matthew 26:42–44, Luke 22:43–44

AFTER THE LORD had torn himself away from the last three disciples as well and gone deeper into the dark shadows of the garden, his fear and agony of soul mounted to its peak. He sank down into the dust, with his face touching the ground, so that from now on the lament of the psalmist, "I am a worm, and no man" (Ps. 22:6) sounds to us like the cry of the Lord. He sees no help anywhere: the disciples are asleep, heaven is closed, and the Father himself seems not to hear his Son. Alone, he wrestles with death and weeps with loud cries. He is bathed in the sweat of fear, and even sweats blood. But he does not leave off. He clings to the Father and holds to him firmly with his prayer, repeated three times. Only an angel is permitted to take pity on him and come down to strengthen him who is Lord of all angels and eternal King.

Who can solve the mystery of this dreadful spiritual struggle? There is a key to it in the words spoken earlier by the Good Shepherd, "No one takes my life from me, but I lay it down of my own accord!" (John 10:18). He was to suffer and die voluntarily. The world could be redeemed and the Father's counsel carried out only if he made this terrible sacrifice of his own free will. We suffer, we die, because we have to. But he had to want – to want of himself – what stood in the crassest opposition to his whole nature.

He who is life had to will to die. The Lord over all the legions of angels had to succumb to the Prince of Darkness. The Son had to wish to be cast off by the judgment of the Father's wrath. That was the tremendous task that had to be accomplished through this prayer battle. And he did accomplish it. First of all he cried out, shuddering, "My Father, if it be possible, let this cup pass from me." Nevertheless, he submitted himself deeply to his Father's will, saying, "Not as I will, but as you will."

In the second prayer he takes a great step forward, "If it is not possible, your will be done." And when he says the same words for the third time with complete surrender and holy tranquility, his Father's will has become wholly his will. Now, at last, he has taken the burden upon his shoulders which at first threatened to crush him, under which he had staggered like one about to collapse. Now he stands upright once more and with a firm step goes toward his goal, ready to suffer all things and endure all things, in perfect obedience and perfect love until the sacrifice is completed.

But we fall down before our exalted Savior, clasp his knees, and beg him to give us his strength and his spirit for two great tasks. Firstly, that we learn to want what God wills: to bear what God lays upon us, to sacrifice what he takes, to die when he calls us. Secondly, that we learn to pray as Christ prayed until we experience, as Christ experienced it, that we are heard – for he was heard beyond all asking when he ascended out of night and death to the glory of the Father.

35

Saturday Morning

The Disciples Sleep

And he came and found them sleeping, and he said to Peter,
"Simon, are you asleep? Could you not watch one hour?
Watch and pray that you may not enter into temptation.
The spirit indeed is willing, but the flesh is weak."... And he
came the third time and said to them, "Are you still sleeping
and taking your rest? It is enough; the hour has come. The
Son of Man is betrayed into the hands of sinners. Rise, let us
be going; see, my betrayer is at hand."

Mark 14:37–42

NOTHING SHOULD have affected and shaken the
disciples more than that their Master in his suffering
of soul sought solace in their love and prayer. He said
pleadingly to them, "My soul is very sorrowful, even
to death; remain here, and watch with me" (Matt.
26:38). But the disciples did not watch and pray; they
sank deeper and deeper into physical exhaustion and

spiritual laziness. It is hard to understand their behavior. They did love their Lord. They saw his anguish of soul; yet they slept while he lay in the dust and struggled with death. He came back to them again and again from his solitary place of prayer, woke them and – cut to the quick – said to Peter, "Simon, are you asleep?" and to all, "Could you not watch one hour with me?" But they slept on and were only half awakened by the Master's loud cry of grief, so that for the third time he found them overcome with sleep. This unnatural sleep was brought about by the kingdom of darkness and gave an indication of the reason for the denial that followed. But the Lord did not reject the poor disciples. On the contrary, he spoke to them full of sympathy and gentleness, "Are you still sleeping and taking your rest? The spirit is willing, but the flesh is weak."

At this time of Lent and throughout our whole lives, he urgently exhorts us saying, "Remain here and watch with me! Watch and pray that you may not enter into temptation!" To be sure, we can watch when it is a matter of our pleasure or our work, and we can watch over our sick ones. But can we hold out even for an hour in unbroken devotion, watching and praying by him who struggled and bled for us and who still continues to seek us today? Most of us find that too difficult! We sleep just as the first disciples did. How lethargic we are in the fight with sin, how lukewarm in love to the Lord, how feeble and distracted in prayer! The enemy of souls seeks to destroy us, death comes nearer and nearer, and we remain sunk in spiritual laziness and bodily ease. This is a soul-murdering sleep, a precursor of eternal death.

But the compassionate Lord will not let us perish in this spiritual sleep. He wants to wake us and asks us again and again through his Word or through blows of fate, "Simon, are you asleep?" And when at long last we are horrified at ourselves and are ready to awake, he lets us see his torment that night, and like lightning the word "For you!" lights up our soul. That must drive the sleep out of our limbs, humble us in repentance and gratitude, and stimulate us to fight for purification. Then the fruits of his struggle with death will fall to us, too. The fear of death that has always accompanied us and embittered everything will disappear. The blessing of a life of prayer will pervade us, and victory over the power and cunning of Satan will crown us.

36

Saturday Evening

Whom Do You Seek?

And immediately, while he was still speaking, Judas came, one of the twelve, and with him a crowd with swords and clubs, from the chief priests and the scribes and the elders.

Then Jesus, knowing all that would happen to him, came forward and said to them, "Whom do you seek?" They answered him, "Jesus of Nazareth."

Mark 14:43; John 18:4–5

JESUS HAD OVERCOME in his struggle. Fear was left behind him; his prayer had been heard. He had prayed that God's will might be done, and he had gained courage and strength to accomplish and to suffer this will. He stood up strengthened, and with the disciples, who at last were awake, went to meet the approaching hostile crowd.

The clang of weapons and the light of torches press their way into the garden. Roman soldiers and Jewish temple guards, led by Judas the traitor and some of the leaders of the people, fill the holy place. The man who was just sweating blood, lying on his face on the ground, stands there unarmed, with quiet majesty in the midst of the armed guards. But they do not dare to seize him. It is as though they are paralyzed by his calm majesty. Then he asks them, "Whom do you seek?" He himself has to make them open their mouths, and though they come with hostile intent they give the right answer: "Jesus of Nazareth."

As the Lord had once asked John and Andrew on their first encounter, "Whom do you seek? What are you seeking?" (John 1:38), so now he asks his enemies surrounding him. God asks the same question of the world and its children throughout all ages, by means of his Spirit and his Word. Human life is a daily search. Many don't know that they are seeking, or what they are seeking, but everyone is seeking something. Anyone who no longer seeks has given up hope, and whoever has given up hope is dead.

Who or what are you looking for? Health, wealth, peace in heart and home? Or help in need, comfort in suffering? Or satisfaction in learned scholarship and science, in the enjoyment of art, in the heights of power? Know that all these things are not the true goal of your search. In all of these you are actually seeking perfect happiness. But you will never find them in the things of this world, in the achievements of your own strength. What you need above all is peace of conscience and victorious life in the midst of death. And more than that: you must find the source of all things including your very being – the living, personal God – as your gracious, compassionate Father in heaven. If you really want to find him, to live and move in him, then seek him who asked the guards, "Whom are you seeking?"

Jesus of Nazareth, the Son of God, the Savior of the world is the deepest and final answer to all human seeking and longing. He is the final answer to all the questions of world history and of the nations, to all the investigation and research of the world's wisdom, and to all the problems of your life. Whoever has found Jesus has a clear conscience, peace of heart, and eternal life. Whoever has found Jesus has found his God and Father and so has found everything. For no one comes to the Father but by him. Seek Jesus and his light; everything else is of no help to you.

Third Week of Lent

37

Sunday Morning

I Am He

Jesus said to them, "I am he." Judas, who betrayed him, was standing with them. When Jesus said to them, "I am he," they drew back and fell to the ground. So he asked them again, "Whom do you seek?" And they said, "Jesus of Nazareth."

John 18:5–7

AFTER THE GUARDS had answered the Lord's question, "Whom do you seek?" by answering, "Jesus of Nazareth," he said to them, "I am he." That was a simple confession, but the battle-hardened men drew back and fell to the ground. What produced this effect? It was first of all the power of truth. So this man was really the wonderful prophet, highly praised but now persecuted to death. The very fact that he fearlessly confessed, "I am he," called forth respect in the mercenaries. Then there was the strength of his personality. The weight of any given word is very different according to the person who speaks it. What a difference there is if it is a coward or a hero, a beggar or a king who says, "I am he." Important men have often done great things simply by their bearing or by their word. But who can be compared with Jesus? Here the influence of personality and the truth of the declaration are combined with a wonderful divine authority, through which the hardened warriors are now thrown to the ground – just as Saul would be later on the road to Damascus. A beam of divine majesty shines forth from these words of the abased Son of Man, and they bear witness to friend and foe throughout all time that he goes to death voluntarily: as he himself has said, "No one takes my life from me, but I lay it down of my own accord" (John 10:18).

At the same time we see that it is a simple thing for the Lord to cast his enemies to the ground if he wants to do so. The might of light over darkness is evident. From now on this "I am he" sounds through the centuries wherever the Lord makes his personal intervention felt in the fortunes of his kingdom or of individual disciples. It rings out, judging and victorious, to the consternation of his enemies and the joy of those who believe in him. One day when all is accomplished, the words will ring out once more over the rubble of the old world in the glory of the transfigured world with creative power: "I am he. I make all things new" (Rev. 21:5).

So we rejoice to find summed up in these few words what the Lord has testified about himself and through his Spirit's might has engraved on our hearts. Out of these words, "I am he," we hear an echo of his testimony of himself: "I am the light of the world" (John 8:12), "I am the bread from heaven" (John 6:51), "I am the resurrection and the life" (John 11:25), "I am the Alpha and the Omega, the beginning and the end, who is and who was and who is to come" (Rev. 1:8). What a comfort for his people! What an encouraging effect it had on that stormy night as the disciples were battling with the waves, when the Lord approached them saying, "Take heart, it is I. Do not be afraid" (Matt. 14:27). It sounded like heavenly music in the hearts of the despondent disciples on Easter evening, when the Risen One appeared in their midst and said, "Peace be with you! Why are you troubled? It is I myself" (Luke 24:36–39).

In the same way, my soul, it should comfort and strengthen your faith when you hear the gospel proclaimed, when you receive the bread and wine, when waves of distress rush upon you, or when the sun shines above you. Finally, when the angel of death draws near, you should hear the blessed words again and again, "I am he."

38

Sunday Evening

The Disciples' Safeguard

Jesus answered, "I told you that I am he. So, if you seek me, let these men go." This was to fulfill the word that he had spoken: "Of those whom you gave me I have lost not one."

John 18:8–9

WHEN, FOR THE SECOND TIME, the Lord asked the guards who were still lying on the ground, "Whom do you seek?" they recovered their senses, arose, and answered once more, "Jesus of Nazareth." Then the Lord gave himself up as a prisoner and at the same time performed another wonder of his might. When he said, "If you seek me, let these men go," he was holding his hand over his disciples, sheltering them. That was not a request; it was a command, and the warriors had to obey the unarmed man. With his word alone, he protected his own from all the power and violence of the enemies. His disciples were not yet capable of suffering with him. First he had to suffer and die for them. Later they would drink of his cup of suffering and be baptized with his baptism of blood, but now he protected them from the outward and physical danger that threatened them. At the same time he saved their souls, as John adds, "This was to fulfill the word which he had spoken: 'Of those whom you gave me I have lost not one.'" As yet the apostles were not able to bear prison and death with the Lord. On that night of stumbling they might actually have fallen away completely from the Lord and so been lost forever. Christ spoke his kingly word, "Let these men go," to yet other powers than those armed henchmen. His eye alone saw behind them the threatening horde from the kingdom of darkness pressing forward to devour his poor disciples. With his command he drove all these powers back and cast them to the ground. The disciples had now the warrant that protected them until the risen Lord gathered them once more around himself and their faith was so strengthened that they were joyfully able to endure torture and death.

"Let these men go" – this is an important word in world history. It is fulfilled in the whole history of the kingdom and is spread like a mighty shield over the disciples of every century against both human and satanic enemies. Under the protection of this shield the first Christian church leaves the old Jerusalem and immigrates safely to places of refuge, and under it the souls of the martyrs go to the heavenly Jerusalem. Under this shield Paul sets out into the heathen world, and a host of missionaries follow him. Without this protection no human being would be saved. Blessed is the man who puts his trust in it.

This word applies to you also, my soul. When temptations rise up against you, your sins terrify you, the accuser accuses you, and the law condemns you, then the Lord's word, "Let these go," is your shield against the fiery arrows of the evil one and will one day be your permit to enter the city of God.

39

Monday Morning

Judas's Kiss

Now the betrayer had given them a sign, saying, "The one I will kiss is the man; seize him." And he came up to Jesus at once and said, "Greetings, Rabbi!" And he kissed him. Jesus said to him, "Friend, why are you here?"

Matthew 26:48–50

WHILE THE GUARDS were still hesitating to lay their rough hands on Jesus, Judas stepped up and kissed him. That was the sign they had agreed on. The kiss is a symbol of friendship and love. Here, however, it was desecrated to be a sign of betrayal. Throughout the Christian world Judas's kiss is regarded as an infamous, hellish crime and the name Judas is the embodiment of all that is accursed.

The betrayal of a king by one of his subjects is detestable. But this case is more than a king and his subject; it is the heavenly redeemer and his chosen disciple, who has now become his betrayer and the leader of his enemies. In the same way apostates often head the persecutors. Judas is no longer led by man but by Satan, and with the kiss he puts the seal on his hatred of Christ. How blind he has become, thinking that the Master cannot see through him and imagining that with his accomplished hypocrisy he can keep up the appearance of being a disciple! The Lord endures a new humiliation by allowing himself to be kissed and feels a pain that burns more than the violence of the enemies – anguish for the lost son. The Savior's gentleness, with which he tries to awaken the dead conscience of the unhappy man, is worthy of adoration: "Friend, why are you here?" But these words can no longer help Judas. They push him toward the abyss into which he will soon sink.

Here we see what wickedness the human heart is capable of and to what lengths a disciple of Christ can go when he abandons the first love and gives himself over to sin and Satan. In all hypocrisy and untruthfulness we recognize the secret beginnings of Judas's sin: when people cover evil desires with pious words; when they flatter their neighbors while inwardly wishing them ill; when a man caresses his wife while desiring someone else. These are steps on the way to eternal destruction. With shame and remorse we look into our own hearts and plead for strength to turn around and for our hearts to be renewed. May we never forget that every time we read the Gospels, attend a worship service, or take part in the Lord's Supper, the Lord asks us the question of conscience, "My friend, why are you here?" May we then be able to say with complete truthfulness, "Lord, I give myself to you."

Peter's Sword

Then Simon Peter, having a sword, drew it and struck the high priest's servant and cut off his right ear. The servant's name was Malchus.

Then Jesus said to him, "Put your sword back into its place. For all who take the sword will perish by the sword."

And he touched his ear and healed him.

John 18:10; Matthew 26:52; Luke 22:51

AFTER THE BETRAYER'S KISS, the guards began to lay hold of Jesus. A servant of the high priest called Malchus was particularly eager. In great agitation the apostles asked their Master, "Lord, shall we strike with the sword?" (Luke 22:49). Before he could answer them, Peter struck at Malchus and cut off his right ear. In this action we see once more the warm love, ardent courage, and vigorous action of the man called "The Rock."

Unfortunately, we also see his haste, his thoughtlessness, and his unspiritual mind. The daring deed of love might have been able to comfort the Lord in his dark night, had not the disciple's lack of understanding and unbroken self-will added a bitter drop to Jesus' cup of suffering.

Peter, still dazed by his heavy sleep and not understanding his Master's purpose, now wanted to fulfill his promise of loyalty. So he hit out wildly. It did not occur to him that he was increasing his Lord's suffering and defiling his cause by making him appear to be the instigator of a brawl. In the midst of these events, the Lord earnestly rebuked his hotheaded disciple, saying, "Put your sword into its sheath; for all who take the sword will perish by the sword." And once more he revealed his glory, for he put right the damage that had been done and, with compassion, healed Malchus's ear.

It is the sacred duty of Christians to take this important teaching to heart in all their struggles. Christ's cause, his kingdom, and his truth can never be defended or furthered by means of physical weapons, violence, coercion, or bloodshed. Such means simply desecrate what is holy. How terribly those who claim to be followers of Peter have sinned against this principle, and what damage has been caused by religious wars!

On the other hand, it has become the norm for subjects to resort to violence against their governments when they think that they are wrongfully treated. All this increases the power of darkness.

We find it hard to hold still when we suffer wrongfully; we would love to knock down our opponent. Let us remember that the holy fight for the Lord and his church is not waged with violence but with watching and praying. It will not be led to victory with weapons of the flesh but with the sword of the Spirit, the Word of God.

41

Tuesday Morning

It Must Be So

*Do you think that I cannot appeal to my Father, and he will
at once send me more than twelve legions of angels? But how
then should the Scriptures be fulfilled, that it must be so?*

Matt. 26:53–54

IN THE MIDST OF THE NOISE, the light of torches
and the clank of weapons, the Lord remained composed. After his rebuke, he said to Peter, "Shall I not
drink the cup which the Father has given me?" (John
18:11). He had accepted the cup from his Father's
hand – the cup from which he had at first drawn back
shuddering – and had made up his mind to empty it. It
was now his own will to do this: no other power could
have compelled him to do so. At the same time he saw
in spirit the shining throngs of angels awaiting a sign
from him to surround and protect him. Aware of this
power, he said to Peter, "Do you think that I cannot

appeal to my Father, and he will at once send me more than twelve legions of angels?" But for our sakes he dispensed with the service of the heavenly hosts, and continued, "But how then should the Scriptures be fulfilled, that it must be so?" This wondrous "must" is the "must" of the unalterable divine purpose and of the prophecies laid down in Holy Scripture.

The Lord is conscious of all the prophetic sayings which must find their fulfillment in his person. He remembers Isaiah's words about the lamb that is led to the slaughter (Isa. 53:7). He knows that he is not only the Good Shepherd (John 10:11) but also the Lamb of God that must be presented as an atoning sacrifice to redeem the world (John 1:29). But this "must" is not brought about by any external force. It is the inner "must" of voluntary obedience, of his own will, of holy love. Thus there is perfect harmony in his whole being when he surrenders to the enemy and forbids his disciples to resist.

"It must be so." We should take that to heart, too, when we feel angry and disheartened by the persecution, need, and ignominy that the church of Christ has to suffer. Then let us remember that it is prophesied in Holy Scripture, in accordance with God's decree, that the church of Christ is to be the follower of her Master, and here on earth she is and will remain a church of the cross. Her participation in Christ's suffering will bring her honor, and thus her way will go through tribulation to glory.

"It must be so." May this also comfort us when we personally suffer injustice and have to bear much pain. We should not rebel against it, but neither should we silently submit to it as an iron necessity. On the contrary, we should recognize our heavenly Father's compassionate love drawing us in this way into the discipleship of our Lord Jesus Christ, and preparing us for eternal happiness. Then we will have strength to bear all things and overcome all things and say to the tempter, "Shall I not drink the cup which the Father has given me?" Then we will experience that the heavenly legions surround and protect us, that the cross strengthens our faith, and that the sufferings of this present time are not worth comparing with the glory that is to be revealed to us (Rom. 8:18).

42

Tuesday Evening

The Arrest

At that hour Jesus said to the crowds, "Have you come out as against a robber, with swords and clubs to capture me? Day after day I sat in the temple teaching, and you did not seize me. But all this has taken place that the Scriptures of the prophets might be fulfilled." Then all the disciples left him and fled.

Matthew 26:55–56

ON THE NIGHT OF THE BETRAYAL several of the leaders of the people accompanied the guards to Gethsemane in order to gloat over the capture of the Lord. The hour had come for the Holy One to be numbered with the transgressors (Isa. 53:12) and delivered up into the hands of sinners. Surrendered to his Father's will, he was ready to let himself be captured; but he was deeply conscious of the injustice and outrage of this violent deed. He protested with dignity and earnestly exhorted the whole hostile crowd to repent – an exhortation that will sound into eternity.

He reminded them that he had been daily with them in the temple and had proclaimed to them the word of truth and of salvation. He had wanted to gather the children of Jerusalem under his wings (Matt. 23:37). Rivers of living water had flowed from him (John 4:10), and thousands had listened to him and hailed him. Now he confronted them with their malice (because already then they would have liked to silence him) and for their cowardice in not daring to arrest him under those circumstances. He also implied that they could not have done it earlier, for the hour appointed by the Father had not come. Then he pronounced judgment over them: "This is your hour, and the power of darkness" (Luke 22:53). Now, in accordance with God's purpose, the time had come when they were permitted to carry out their deed of violence, and the kingdom of darkness was allowed to deploy all its might against the Lord.

With those words he revealed to them that they were themselves children of that kingdom and tools of Satan and that with this deed they would be completely fettered by him. We can see in these embittered enemies how dark the human heart can become when it is hardened in unbelief and yields to Satan.

Then the Lord let himself be bound by the guards and led away as a prisoner. The disciples, however, all left him and fled. Their flight was a sad testimony to their weakness. But it was also prophesied and desired by the Lord, for it was his will to walk the road to death deserted and alone. He wanted to atone, suffer, and die for all – alone. He went in chains to free his people from their bondage to sin and from death and judgment and to grant them the glorious freedom of the children of God.

How easily do we too become unfaithful to the Lord when the world lures or threatens us. But he does not give up working on our souls so that at last we may experience that if the Son sets us free we will be free indeed (John 8:36).

43

Wednesday Morning

Christ before Annas

First they led him to Annas, for he was the father-in-law of Caiaphas, who was high priest that year. It was Caiaphas who had advised the Jews that it would be expedient that one man should die for the people. . . . The high priest then questioned Jesus about his disciples and his teaching. Jesus answered him, "I have spoken openly to the world. I have always taught in synagogues and in the temple, where all Jews come together. I have said nothing in secret. Why do you ask me? Ask those who have heard me what I said to them; they know what I said." When he had said these things, one of the officers standing by struck Jesus with his hand, saying, "Is that how you answer the high priest?" Jesus answered him, "If what I said is wrong, bear witness about the wrong; but if what I said is right, why do you strike me?"

John 18:13–14, 19–23

PERHAPS JUDAS remained behind in Gethsemane, watching benumbed the departure of the torchlit procession, while within his soul the worm that does not die began to gnaw. But Jesus was led away, bound by the soldiers. They did not know what they were doing; they were probably disconcerted now that they had captured him. But he walked calmly with them back to Jerusalem, to the palace of the high priest.

He was brought first to Annas, the former high priest. This wily old man was supposed to draw out from the prisoner some reason for the sentence which had already been decided. That is why he questioned him about his disciples and his teaching, in an attempt to brand him in the eyes of the Romans as a leader of rebels, and in the eyes of the Jews as a false prophet. But the Lord said nothing about his disciples, whom he had released under his protection. He pointed out how publicly he had taught and the thousands who had heard him—an answer so magnificent that the hypocritical judge was quite at a loss. Then, in order to win his commander's favor, an insolent servant struck God's Holy One in the face with a threatening shout. The Lord did not cause his hand to wither but answered him with great gentleness in order to bring him to his senses: "If what I said is wrong, bear witness about the wrong; but if what I said is right, why do you strike me?" He left vengeance to God (Rom 12:19) and presented not only the other cheek to his enemies (Matt. 5:39) but his whole body to be crucified.

Annas, Caiaphas, and the others were priests. The darkest page of history bears witness against the priesthood. Later the priests of Rome would follow that sinister example by persecuting heretics and burning them at the stake. Alas, how would the Lord Christ be treated even by many churches if he were to appear again as a carpenter's son surrounded by fishermen and tax collectors, proclaiming his decisive and revolutionary teaching openly without being ordained, without asking about the dogmas of the theologians and the instructions of the clergy?

Here all who wear the vestments of the clergy in any form have to repent deeply. They should look into their hearts and test before God what they are seeking in their office: Christ or themselves, Christ's truth or their own opinion, Christ's honor or their own reputation? True servants of Christ should be ashamed of the anger that rises within them when they are mistreated. They should learn gentleness from the Lord and consider that, through the slap Christ suffered, all the enemies' blows have lost their bitterness. They are consecrated as part of following Christ.

44

Wednesday Evening

The False Witness

Then those who had seized Jesus led him to Caiaphas the high priest, where the scribes and the elders had gathered.... Now the chief priests and the whole council were seeking false testimony against Jesus that they might put him to death, but they found none, though many false witnesses came forward.

Matthew 26:57, 59–60

THE LORD CHRIST STANDS THERE, bound, before the highest court of justice, which has been called to a meeting by night. But what a moral abyss opens up here. The council is determined to keep up a form of justice. A trial is instituted. The accused is to be questioned and a legal sentence passed. But even before the interrogation, the judges have decided that this man must die because he stands in the way of their reputation and their power. He has told them the truth relentlessly, and the people hang on to him. He must be gotten rid of, but under the semblance of the law. The most malicious and fateful judicial murder of world history is decided upon. False witnesses have been hired in advance.

Woe to a nation that produces such judges, that lets itself be led by such leaders! Woe to a land where the representatives of the law persecute truth and right, where Christ and his kingdom are sentenced to death with lying testimony, while criminals like Barabbas are acquitted. Then storm clouds will gather and the lightning of divine judgment do its work – as the smoking ruins of Jerusalem proclaim to all ages.

Now, does the council achieve its purpose with the hired witnesses? Not at all. Their testimonies do not agree. They contradict one another and so serve to place the innocence of the silent Jesus in the brightest light. "Which one of you convicts me of sin?" the Lord had once asked (John 8:46). Here in his passion the answer is given. His most malicious enemies can produce no proof against him. They only frustrate one another. That is always the outcome of false testimony against the gospel.

In every age the gospel has had embittered enemies. It has been attacked and slandered, but repeatedly "their testimony did not agree." The church of Christ always comes to new strength. The persecutions of the enemy have only served to place her imperishable worth into still brighter light.

Following the example of her Master, her way is and will always be the way of the cross. It leads through darkness into light. An important proof of the truth of Christianity continues to be the mutual disagreement of her enemies and their untenable, contradictory teachings. The urgent challenge goes out to all Christians, to give a shining testimony to the Lord by leading a holy life. For it was on account of their sins that he was willing to be silent before his false judges.

45

Thursday Morning

Jesus' Silence

And the high priest stood up in the midst and asked Jesus, "Have you no answer to make? What is it that these men testify against you?" But he remained silent and made no answer.

Mark 14:60–61

JUST JUDGES would have punished the false witnesses severely, but these leaders had themselves hired them. In the excitement of that black night they had neglected to coach the paid liars so that their statements would agree. The witnesses come forward, one after the other, becoming entangled in their lies. Their false testimonies contradict each other so that not even these judges can find a valid accusation, still less produce proof of guilt. Meanwhile Jesus stands still and silent. Certainly, there is power in speech. What effects men have produced through their words! Above all, what an influence Christ exercised through his proclamation of the gospel! But there is also a great power in silence. There is a time for speech and a time for silence (Eccles. 3:7). It takes great wisdom and strength to be silent at the right time, and at the right time to say the right word. Christ possessed this quality in the greatest measure. As long as he still hoped to win souls through the word of truth and to call hardened sinners to repentance, he spoke. When he kept silence now before these judges, who knew he was innocent but who had no ear for truth and no conscience, it was a terrible silence of judgment.

Here begins the fulfillment of the prophecy of the silent lamb that is led to the slaughter and is dumb before its shearers (Isa. 53:7). It is also the fulfillment of the words of the psalm: "I must be as a mute man who does not open his mouth. . . . But for you, O Lord, do I wait; it is you, O Lord my God, who will answer" (Ps. 38:13, 15).

This silence, which involves quiet submission and holy judgment, is one of the most sublime things that we encounter on the Lord's way of the cross. With majesty the fettered man stands in the midst of disunited witnesses and agitated judges. What power he wields with this silence! His enemies feel themselves rebuked and judged and give way to anger and confusion. But the Lord guides the whole meeting toward the goal it has to reach in accordance with his will and his own free confession.

The Lord's holy silence should be an incisive call to repentance to us Christians. It should remind us of the sins that we have committed through the destructive misuse of speech and of the harm that we have done with our thoughtless, false, and angry words. Then the silently suffering Savior will draw us into his discipleship with his noble example. He will help us to become strong in quietness and hope, and with gentleness to overcome the world.

46

Thursday Evening

Christ's Confession

And the high priest said to him, "I adjure you by the living God, tell us if you are the Christ, the Son of God." Jesus said to him, "You have said so. But I tell you, from now on you will see the Son of Man seated at the right hand of Power and coming on the clouds of heaven."

Matthew 26:62–64

GOD'S HOLY ONE was still standing before the judicial assembly called together that night. His continued silence increased the confusion and irritation of the leaders of Israel. They began to fear that their plan to kill their victim under the pretext of law might come to nothing. Then Caiaphas arose, a man with a will of iron and of ruthlessness, in order to get himself and his companions out of the embarrassing situation. He was the high priest, and now against his will he became an instrument in the hand of God.

He recalled how often Jesus had spoken of himself as the Son of God, and that the scribes had already accused him of blasphemy for this reason. The penalty for blasphemy was death. So Caiaphas gave up the circuitous ways of cunning and steered straight to the goal. If Jesus would now acknowledge what he had formerly stated, the reason for the death penalty would be found. But he stood there so silently – would he deign to give his enemies an answer? Here too Caiaphas knew what to do. He put the matter under oath, saying solemnly, "I adjure you by the living God, tell us if you are the Christ, the Son of God?"

A historic moment has come. The answer has already been given in the predictions of the prophets, in the testimonies of heaven, and in the Lord's teachings and miracles. Nevertheless, the Lord will remain silent no longer. He knows that his answer will plunge him into the most cruel death. But he cannot evade the oath placed before him. The Son of God cannot deny himself. He cannot and will not keep silence in answer to the greatest question confronting humanity. He cannot and will not leave his present and future disciples in doubt as to who and what he is. So he now opens his silent lips and confirms before heaven and earth, "It is as you say. I am." This declaration judges the lack of faith of all ages. At the same time it is the source from which springs the joyful confession of his disciples: "I believe that Jesus Christ, true God, begotten of the Father from eternity, and also true man, born of the Virgin Mary, is my Lord."

Then, while perhaps a gleam of transfiguration passes over his face, the Lord adds to his declaration the sublime prophecy, "From now on you will see the Son of Man seated at the right hand of Power, and coming on the clouds of heaven!" The judges who now condemn the Son of Man will see him again as the exalted Son of God. One day they will see him coming as the judge of all worlds – and as their judge – in the ruins of this earth. How will it be with them then? As for us, we plead that we may have the eyes of Stephen so that we, enlightened by the Holy Spirit, may in faith see heaven open and the Son of Man seated as our Savior at the right hand of God.

47

Friday Morning

The Death Sentence

Then the high priest tore his robes and said, "He has uttered blasphemy. What further witnesses do we need? You have now heard his blasphemy. What is your judgment?" They answered, "He deserves death." Then they spit in his face and struck him. And some slapped him, saying, "Prophesy to us, you Christ! Who is it that struck you?"

Matthew 26:65–68

WHEN THE LORD CONFESSED that he was the Christ, the elders of Israel should have fallen on their knees before him and thanked him with tears of joy. The Messiah, proclaimed by the prophets and longed for by all the devout in Israel had come at last to redeem his people and to fulfill Jehovah's gracious promises. Instead, the high priest tore his robes in hypocritical indignation and said, "He has uttered blasphemy.

What further witnesses do we need? You have heard his blasphemy. What is your judgment?"

The leaders of Israel may have considered for a moment, but not a voice was raised in favor of their prisoner. Nicodemus and Joseph of Arimathea were certainly not present. Perhaps they had not been called to the meeting at all for fear of their disagreement. Then the first judge opened his mouth and said, "He deserves death!" and one after the other repeated the verdict in horrible blindness: "He deserves death!" The death sentence was unanimously pronounced.

This fact stands in the center of world history. The King of Israel is condemned to death by the elders of his nation, the Son of God by the children of man, and the Holy One by the sinners whom he came to save. It is a verdict that cries to heaven when we consider the wicked judges who pronounce it and God's Holy One on whom it is passed. It is nevertheless a just verdict, for the terrible sentence sounds from the throne of the eternal Judge as well: "He deserves death!" Death is the wages of sin, and Christ is made sin for us. He stands on trial in place of us and vouches for us with his blood. So it is over you and me and all of us sinners that the sentence is here pronounced: "He deserves death." That should tear off our cloak of vanity and self-righteousness and show us who and what we are in God's sight. That should startle and shock us, pull us down on our knees, and force from the depth of our souls the cry, "Mercy! Mercy! Lord, have mercy! Christ, have mercy!"

But if we have arrived at this point, then nothing in heaven or on earth can console and uplift us as much as that sentence of death passed and carried out upon our Redeemer. For all our guilt and condemnation is taken from us and cast on him. In his sentence the whole severity of perfect justice and the unfathomable compassion of eternal love toward lost humanity are combined. Now we should press through to the assurance of faith that we are really free from guilt and punishment and that no judgment condemns us anymore. From this time onwards death has lost its sting, for to us it is no longer death but the entrance into eternal life.

Whereas at that time the cruel judges mocked the innocent prisoner, spat at him, and struck him with their fists, we today lift our eyes to the exalted head of the church and with ardent thanks call out, "Blessed be your glorious name in all eternity!"

48

Friday Evening

Peter's Fall

And as Peter was below in the courtyard, one of the servant girls of the high priest came, and seeing Peter warming himself, she looked at him and said, "You also were with the Nazarene, Jesus." But he denied it, saying, "I neither know nor understand what you mean." And he went out into the gateway and the rooster crowed. And the servant girl saw him and began again to say to the bystanders, "This man is one of them." But again he denied it. And after a little while the bystanders again said to Peter, "Certainly you are one of them, for you are a Galilean." But he began to invoke a curse on himself and to swear, "I do not know this man of whom you speak."

Mark 14:66–71

PETER AND JUDAS were opposite natures – one closed, hypocritical, and self-centered; the other open, frank, and dedicated to the Lord. Peter also fell deeply, but it was possible for him to rise again. There were three stages that led to his shameful denial: false self-confidence, spiritual sleepiness, and disobedience to the Lord. "Even though they all fall away, I will not. I am ready to go to prison and to death with you," he had declared (Matt. 26:33; Luke 22:33). With this pledge he had cast the Master's warning to the winds and placed himself above the other disciples. True, the urge behind this vow was warm love; but his trust was only in his own heart. "Whoever trusts in his own mind is a fool" (Prov. 28:26). Pride goes before a fall (Prov. 16:18).

When the Lord was wrestling with death in Gethsemane, Peter slept as the others did. How sadly the Savior's question rings, "Could you not watch with me one hour?" (Matt. 26:40). But alas, they continued to sleep – physically and spiritually – until the traitor appeared and the hour of sifting struck. Anyone who sleeps like that is easily ensnared by the tempter. Wherever the Lord's warning, "Watch and pray!" is not followed, a fall is near. Peter did pull himself together when he drew his sword, but he did so as in a wild dream. He proved his daring, but by wielding the weapon of the flesh he forgot what manner of spirit he was (Luke 9:55). Soon his courage changed to timidity and he fled like the others.

Remembering his promise, he did turn back, it is true. He slunk after the Master and pressed his way into the high priest's courtyard. But in doing this, he was disobedient, for the Lord had expressly said to him, "You cannot follow me now" (John 13:36).

As he sat in the courtyard, warming himself with the guards at the fire, he gave in to the fear of men, and denied his beloved Master. He was recognized by his speech. In the same way the children of God are always recognized by their words and behavior, and there is nothing more shameful than when they act against their conscience like the children of the world.

While the Lord goes to death for his disciples, Peter denies him three times! He had once said enthusiastically, "Lord, to whom shall we go? You have the words of eternal life, and we have believed and come to know that you are Christ, the Son of the living God" (John 6:68–69). Yet now that his Master is condemned to death, he curses and swears, "I do not know the man."

Should we now sit in judgment over him? No, if such a man – the rock – fell so deeply, it must have been hard to stand. We remember how often we have also sat at the fire of Christ's enemies, and denied not only our own conviction, not only many friends, but also the

Lord himself. We bow our heads and pray for courage to bear witness to our faith in word and deed.

49

Saturday Morning

Peter's Repentance

And immediately, while he was still speaking, the rooster crowed. And the Lord turned and looked at Peter. And Peter remembered the saying of the Lord, how he had said to him, "Before the rooster crows today, you will deny me three times." And he went out and wept bitterly.

Luke 22:60–62

IT WAS BY THREE STAGES that Peter sank into the depth of his fall, but three lifesaving powers joined to raise him up again. These were his inner relationship with his Master, the cockcrow, and Jesus' divine look.

Despite Peter's stumble, he could not abandon the Lord. His love to him had pressed him into that temptation-laden courtyard. Even when he denied the Lord miserably with his lips, the inner tie of community with him was not dissolved. It had become a thin, invisible thread – another step downward and it would have broken, but that step was not taken, and this thread helped to restore him. Christ's word was fulfilled: "Simon, I have prayed for you that your faith may not fail" (Luke 22:32). To this there came the rousing voice of the cockcrow. It screamed in his ear and struck his heart. Hearing the call, he was reminded of the Lord's warning and grasped the whole extent of his fall with horror. He woke up, appalled at himself.

The Lord never neglects to issue such a rousing call when his children have fallen or are following ways that endanger their souls. Sometimes these calls are inner warnings of conscience, sometimes the remarks of friends or enemies, sometimes words of Holy Scripture, and sometimes what the world calls blows of fate. Like a cockcrow, these calls should rouse the soul. Then everything depends on hearing the call, standing up to it, and judging oneself. Of course the cockcrow alone would not have saved Peter. A higher help had to come, for which the cockcrow was only a preparation.

Once when Peter was about to sink in the waves of the sea, he had called out, "Lord, save me!" (Matt. 14:30), and Jesus' hand had saved him. Now again only the Lord could save his fallen disciple; and it was through his divine look that he did it. What all did it express? First, pain at being forsaken by all his disciples and denied by Peter. Then, sorrow over his disciple's fall and the quiet reproach of hurt love. Finally, this look doubtless said to Peter, "Your guilt is great, but my compassion is still greater. You renounce me, but my love never ends. You deny me, but I consecrate myself to die as a sacrifice for you."

Peter understood the look: it pierced to the depth of his soul. He went out and wept bitterly. The strong man broke down and his tears flowed. The old Simon, son of John, melted in this flood. The divine look of the Lord, however, remained his solace and support. He knew that he had not been cast off. Later he was permitted, though ashamed and sad, to look the Risen One in the face and confess, "Lord, you know everything; you know that I love you" (John 21:17). From then on he could deny no more, but sealed his love to the Lord by martyrdom.

50

Saturday Evening

Judas's End

*Then when Judas, his betrayer, saw that Jesus was con-
demned, he changed his mind and brought back the thirty
pieces of silver to the chief priests and the elders, saying, "I
have sinned by betraying innocent blood." They said, "What
is that to us? See to it yourself." And throwing down the
pieces of silver into the temple, he departed, and he went
and hanged himself.*

Matthew 27:3–5

JUDAS WAS NO INSIGNIFICANT MAN, as the mag-
nitude of his crime shows. The Lord himself had chosen
him to be an apostle, so he must have had a certain
enthusiasm for the Master. But now that was lost in a
terrible way.

The shadows of the darkest night had gone, and
the morning of Good Friday dawned. All had been
decided. Jesus was condemned to death. Then Judas

recovered his senses. Until now he had dulled and suppressed his conscience. It hadn't stirred when he kissed Jesus in the garden; it seemed to be trampled to death. But it was not dead. The more violently it had been suppressed, the more terrible was its present awakening. Its voice became like that of a lion and it roared, "Traitor! Traitor!" at the son of perdition. Where could he go? The thirty pieces of silver burned in his pocket like hellish fire. Driven by the lashes of his conscience, he hurried to the temple and flung the blood money at the priests' feet. As he did so, he testified to the Master whom he had sold: "I have sinned by betraying innocent blood."

Did he expect to receive comfort and sympathy from the Lord's enemies? The elders answered coldly, "What is that to us? See to it yourself."

But didn't Judas's remorse have the promise of grace? Yes, "godly grief produces a repentance that leads to salvation without regret" (2 Cor. 7:10). Peter's sadness was of that kind. He wept over his sin and, guided by the Lord's gracious look, he sought and found forgiveness with him. Grief over sin is transfigured to redeeming repentance only when it is pervaded by faith in forgiving grace. Judas too could have found grace at the cross of his betrayed and dying Master if he had sought and believed it. But he was no longer able to do so – that was the judgment on his hardness of heart. He could no longer believe in God's compassion. His remorse plunged him into the abyss of despair. "Worldly grief produces death" (2 Cor. 7:10). So Judas went and hanged himself.

Over the abyss into which he sinks, the Lord's words resound, "The Son of Man goes as it is written of him, but woe to that man by whom the Son of Man is betrayed! It would have been better for that man if he had not been born" (Matt. 26:24). This pained lament from the lips of the Savior of sinners is more dreadful than all the curses of Sinai.

May Judas's end reveal Satan's terrible snares to all who are fearful, and to anyone who entertains thoughts of suicide. These snares are despondency and despair. So believe that God's grace in Christ is greater than your greatest sin; yes, greater than the sin of the whole world.

Fourth Week of Lent

51

Sunday Morning

Handed Over to the Gentiles

Then they led Jesus from the house of Caiaphas to the gover-
nor's headquarters. It was early morning. They themselves
did not enter the governor's headquarters, so that they
would not be defiled, but could eat the Passover. So Pilate
went outside to them and said, "What accusation do you
bring against this man?" They answered him, "If this man
were not doing evil, we would not have delivered him over
to you." Pilate said to them, "Take him yourselves and
judge him by your own law." The Jews said to him, "It is not
lawful for us to put anyone to death." This was to fulfill the
word that Jesus had spoken to show by what kind of death
he was going to die.

John 18:28–32

THE MORNING OF GOOD FRIDAY had dawned
over Jerusalem. The greatest day in world history, the
turning point of all times, had come. The members of

the council met early in the judgment hall in order to confirm formally the sentence of death, which they had passed on their Messiah that night. However, because they were subjected to the hated yoke of the Romans, they were not allowed to carry out the execution themselves. They had to leave that to the pagan government.

So now they led the Son of David, bound, to the Roman procurator Pontius Pilate. At the time he had his residence in the praetorium, in the proud castle Antonia. In front of it there was a stone pavement or rise in the ground called Gabbatha in Aramaic (John 19:13). Here they handed their prisoner over to the pagan judge. The true king, for whom the nations longed, was rejected by his own people.

In this way the Lord's prophecy that he would be handed over to the Gentiles was fulfilled, and he also became the Savior of the Gentiles. Jews and Gentiles joined to put him to death; Jews and Gentiles from now on can find in him their Redeemer and the source of their joy. All the nations of the earth shall be gathered to his banner. Without wanting to, the poisonous enemies had moved forward God's great plan of salvation for all nations.

The members of the council remained outside in order to avoid "being made unclean" by entering the house of a pagan. The hypocrites believed they were keeping themselves pure by observing their outward regulations; inwardly they fostered lies and thirst for blood. Their evil spirit has not died out, as shown also by the practices of many Christians. They believe that by going to church they are devout, while at home they live in sin.

Finally, those Jewish judges who clamored to get Pilate to ratify the death sentence were given a bitter pill to swallow. He said to them, "Take him and judge him according to your law." They had to confess their powerlessness and their murderous intent: "It is not lawful for us to put any man to death." So the Lord was handed over to the Roman executioners. Thus the prophecy that he would die on a cross was fulfilled, for crucifixion was a Roman means of execution. His holy body was not to be broken by a Jewish stoning, but to be kept unbroken in the tomb until he rose again. Once again divine providence arrived at its long-determined goal. Confidently and in adoration, we too surrender ourselves in life and in death to the eternally wise and gracious leading of our heavenly Father.

52

Sunday Evening

What Have You Done?

Pilate entered his headquarters again and called Jesus and said to him, "Are you the King of the Jews?" Jesus answered, "Do you say this of your own accord, or did others say it to you about me?" Pilate answered, "Am I a Jew? Your own nation and the chief priests have delivered you over to me. What have you done?"

John 18:33–35

TO THE JEWS it was blasphemy and to the Romans agitation for which Jesus deserved the death penalty. That was what the cunning high priests had decided. So they now accused the victim of their hatred before the governor, saying that he had forbidden the payment of taxes to the Roman emperor, and that he had proclaimed himself king. Now Pilate had to take the matter in hand. He led the prisoner into the praetorium to be interrogated, and half sympathetically, half mockingly, asked him, "Are you the King of the Jews?" The Lord looked at the proud Roman and began to work upon the soul of this pagan judge by countering his question with another. Was Pilate asking out of his own deep interest or in his official capacity? He was to consider whether the mystery of Jesus' person and dignity might not have significance for himself.

For us too, the question about the Lord and his work must never become a mere intellectual or official question. We will only receive a saving answer when it has become a burning, vital question to us.

Pilate senses something of the majesty of the prisoner and grows uneasy, but he hastily evades the question by exclaiming, "Am I a Jew?" By this he means to say, "I have nothing to do with you and your religious questions; but as judge I have to investigate your case." Then he continues the interrogation, saying, "What have you done?"

Pilate has no idea of the great significance of the question that he asks with indifference. What an answer the Lord might have given! All the books in the world would not exhaust its content (John 21:25). It would include them all: the paralytics, the blind, the lepers who had been healed; those who had been set free from impure spirits; those who had been raised from the dead; the pardoned sinners; the mourners who had been comforted; and the evildoers who had become God's children. They would have to come from all nations and all times, raise their voices and testify to what the Lord Jesus Christ has done for them and in them. What a psalm that would have been! What harmonies would fill heaven and earth!

Yes, we ourselves have urgent reason to consider deeply what the Lord Christ has done for the whole world and what he has done for us and in us. If our hearts have found the right answer, we must be filled with thanks and adoration and, in word and deed, join in the immortal songs of that blessed choir. At the same time we must not forget to keep on asking ourselves the question, "What have you done?" until, set free from all self-righteousness, in deep shame at the worthlessness of all our actions, we recognize the burden of all that we have done and left undone. We will find in the World Redeemer's deed of love our comfort in life and in death.

53

Monday Morning

The King of Truth

Jesus answered, "My kingdom is not of this world. If my kingdom were of this world, my servants would have been fighting, that I might not be delivered over to the Jews. But my kingdom is not from the world." Then Pilate said to him, "So you are a king?" Jesus answered, "You say that I am a king. For this purpose I was born and for this purpose I have come into the world – to bear witness to the truth. Everyone who is of the truth listens to my voice." Pilate said to him, "What is truth?" After he had said this, he went back outside to the Jews and told them, "I find no guilt in him."

John 18:36–38

AN HOUR OF GRACE and, at the same time, an hour of decision has struck for Pilate. Christ, the king of truth, stands before him and tries to win his soul. Jesus allows the Roman a glimpse into his royal glory, into his kingdom. From the words, "My kingdom is not of this world," Pilate is to see that the accused has done nothing that can be condemned as rebellion against the empire. Further, they reveal a world higher than this earth and that this Jesus really has a kingdom that comes from above. The weapon of this kingdom is not the sword. Its wealth is not gold and its object is not the glory of this world.

When will Christ's disciples learn that their Master's kingdom is not built with the means of this world nor defended with this world's weapons? The success and power of this world are not to be sought in it.

Pilate, however, asks with amazement, "So you are a king?" To this the Lord gives the wonderful answer, "Indeed I am a king," and adds the revelation that his kingdom is the kingdom of truth. Its source is truth. Truth is its wealth and happiness, its power and its goal. The citizens of this kingdom are the children of truth.

Will a breath of longing awaken in Pilate? Will he bow before this king and plead to become a citizen of his kingdom? It may well be that a longing is stirred in him, but he senses that in the light of truth his evil deeds would have to be punished, his old ways and the splendor of this world given up. He does not want that. He can't do it. He loves darkness more than light (John 3:19), he has long since submitted to the pagan maxim, "The only thing that is certain is that nothing is certain." He closes his heart. With a mocking shrug of his shoulders, he calls out to the king of truth, "What is truth?" and turns away from him. He goes out once more and tries vainly to stifle his conscience by testifying, "I find no guilt in him."

We Christians, however, rejoice when the Lord affirms before the religious court that he is the Son of God, and before the secular judge, "I am a king." For that is our consolation and our joy. Yes, he is King of all kings, Lord of all lords (1 Tim. 6:15), and his kingdom is an eternal one. He has accepted us into this kingdom. We bear his name, we stand under his protection, we live from the riches of his grace. One day we will take part in his heavenly blessedness when he comes again to establish the kingdom of his glory. But there is a condition attached to this: we must seek and love his truth. We must follow it unconditionally and serve it joyfully, even though we have to struggle and suffer on account of it. We must bear witness to it in word and deed until he comes.

54

Monday Evening

Jesus before Herod

But they were urgent, saying, "He stirs up the people, teaching throughout all Judea, from Galilee even to this place." When Pilate heard this, he asked whether the man was a Galilean. And when he learned that he belonged to Herod's jurisdiction, he sent him over to Herod, who was himself in Jerusalem at that time. When Herod saw Jesus, he was very glad, for he had long desired to see him, because he had heard about him, and he was hoping to see some sign done by him. So he questioned him at some length, but he made no answer. The chief priests and the scribes stood by, vehemently accusing him. And Herod with his soldiers treated him with contempt and mocked him. Then, arraying him in splendid clothing, he sent him back to Pilate. And Herod and Pilate became friends with each other that very day, for before this they had been at enmity with each other.

Luke 23:5–12

AS SIMEON already prophesied, as soon as people enter the light of the cross of Christ, what is in their innermost heart is revealed (Luke 2:35). We see this in Peter and Judas, in Caiaphas and Pilate. It was also fulfilled in Herod.

When Pilate learned that Jesus came from Galilee, he hoped to be relieved of the irksome matter and sent him to Herod, for Galilee was under his jurisdiction. The true King was brought before the judgment seat of the sham king – another agony on his way to death. Surrounded by soldiers, he had to go again through the streets of Jerusalem as a criminal in fetters and endure the brutalities of hatred. At last he stood before the adulterous prince, the murderer of John the Baptist.

"When Herod saw Jesus, he was very glad." What kind of joy was that? With what jubilation Abraham, Moses, David, and Isaiah would have greeted the longed-for Messiah if they had been privileged to see him. What rapture will fill our souls one day when we see him in his glory! But Herod was glad because he was hoping "to see some sign" done by him. He thought that he could use this man, who now stood as a prisoner before him, as a means to satisfy his curiosity and enliven his boredom. When he had first heard of him, he had sensed a secret dread, but now he hoped to see him do something interesting that would entertain his court. He treated the Lord as a clown and asked him many mocking questions. But Jesus did not answer at all; he remained completely silent until the end.

What words of truth the Lord had had for those seeking salvation, words of comfort for the broken-hearted, words of grace for the repentant, but also what words of judgment for stiff-necked opponents, as long as conversion was still possible! But where he does not answer a single word, he has given up on the questioner; he does not want to give what is holy to dogs or cast pearls before swine (Matt. 7:6). In Jesus' silence there lies the complete condemnation of this royal slave of vice.

In the same way the Lord continues to be silent toward the scoffers of all times and toward the prying questions of curiosity and unbelief. Those who attend the preaching of the gospel only in order to criticize will also receive no answer to their doubting questions as long as they turn a deaf ear to warnings to repent.

While the Lord, suffering and in silence, works for the redemption of the lost world – and so in the eyes of the angels stands there in indescribable beauty – Herod and all his court ridicule him. In mockery they have a white toga put on him, such as was then worn by those seeking a government appointment. The white color was at the same time meant to indicate that Herod regarded him as one innocently accused, an inoffensive harmless man. So he sent him back to Pilate, and from that time the two became friends – to the delight of the archenemy. How will they feel when one day they see the one whom they had scoffed as Judge of the world, robed in shining, heavenly majesty! But even at that hour, the Lord was weaving the white garment of purity and honor for all who believe in him, in which they will be able to stand with joy before the throne of the just Judge one day.

55

Tuesday Morning

The Precipitous Path

Pilate then called together the chief priests and the rulers and the people, and said to them, "You brought me this man as one who was misleading the people. And after examining him before you, behold, I did not find this man guilty of any of your charges against him. Neither did Herod, for he sent him back to us. Look, nothing deserving death has been done by him. I will therefore punish and release him."

Luke 23:13–16

PILATE HAD A SHORT SPELL of peace and quiet in his castle, hoping that Herod would pronounce sentence in this disagreeable case. But that fox did not enter the trap. He sent the prisoner back to the governor. In the meantime, a crowd had gathered to accompany him. With displeasure Pilate became aware of the approaching throng and only too soon received the news that he was not to be spared the verdict.

From the beginning he had recognized Christ's innocence. He had received an impression of the majesty of his person, and he still had the intention to set him free. He was aware, however, of the persistence and rage of the accusers. If he acquitted Jesus, he had to be prepared for the worst complications, perhaps insurrection and bloodshed. His present military force was in all probability too weak to crush a revolution promptly. In addition, he worried that he would be accused and slandered to the distrustful and cruel Emperor Tiberius. Under the influence of these considerations, he entered upon the ruinous path of negotiating with the unscrupulous leaders of the people, of yielding to wrong and of compromising between good and evil. Thus he set out on the precipitous way that was bound at last to plunge him to ruin.

What a criminal half-measure was his verdict, "I will chastise him and let him go!" A clear decision was called for: if guilty, punishment; if innocent, release! Pilate despised the Jews, but did not dare to break with them. He strove for a just verdict, but did not dare to give it. Finally the wretched man thought he would satisfy Christ's enemies by maltreating their victim, and quieten his own conscience by releasing the innocent prisoner after having him flogged. With the promise of chastisement, the unhappy man had taken the fatal step that only too soon would force him to consent to crucifixion.

What damage all do to themselves who deny their better conviction because of the fear of men, who break God's commandment for the sake of the world's favor and sacrifice their inner life for outward well-being! How senseless it is to try to compromise between irreconcilable opposites, between truth and lies, between good and evil! The first step from what is right presses us to take the second and third. Whoever offers evil a finger must soon let it have his whole hand. Such intermediaries deal their consciences deadly blows. They lose their balance of mind and peace of soul. They continue on their way halfheartedly and with broken wills. Their path becomes more and more precipitous. Thinking they are furthering their happiness, they become the most miserable people.

56

Tuesday Evening

The Warning

Now at the feast the governor was accustomed to release for the crowd any one prisoner whom they wanted. And they had then a notorious prisoner called Barabbas. So when they had gathered, Pilate said to them, "Whom do you want me to release for you: Barabbas, or Jesus who is called Christ?" For he knew that it was out of envy that they had delivered him up. Besides, while he was sitting on the judgment seat, his wife sent word to him, "Have nothing to do with that righteous man, for I have suffered much because of him today in a dream."

Matthew 27:15–19

WHILE PILATE WAS NEGOTIATING with the elders, he was asked by the crowd to release a prisoner, as was his custom at the Passover festival. He seized this opportunity to shift the decision of Jesus' fate from himself to the populace. Expecting a favorable answer, he let them choose between the one who had done only good and Barabbas, a murderer.

The whole of Jesus' activity took place during this governor's term of office, so Pilate must have been well informed of all that he did in public, of his royal entry into Jerusalem, and of the great excitement among the people. Doubtless, all these events had also been eagerly discussed in the governor's palace, and his wife Claudia found a keen interest in them. As Pilate was about to take his place on the judgment seat, which was set up on the terrace called Gabbatha, he received a message from his wife: "Have nothing to do with that righteous man, for I have suffered much over him today in a dream."

The fact that she had this dream shows her interest in the matter, her good will, and her anxiety as to how it would end. By daring to interrupt the official activity of the procurator by sending him a private message, she gives proof of her love for her husband and of her longing for a just decision. Every wife may be reminded by this of her task to guard and warn her husband on the temptation-filled way of his calling. Similarly, every husband should learn to be more conscientious in listening to the warning of his faithful wife. If Pilate had followed the warning, what might it have meant for him – especially if he had become a martyr on account of it.

However, there is something still higher to bear in mind. Just as in earlier times the Lord often spoke to people through dreams, this dream was beyond a doubt sent by God. At this decisive moment the Father gave a heavenly testimony for the innocence of his beloved Son. The message from Pilate's wife was a warning that was intended to rouse his conscience. It did have this effect for a moment, but it did not last long.

Today too dreams may contain a reminder for the conscience. Warnings that come to us through friends, enemies, or events in our lives should likewise be accepted and obeyed as rousing calls from God. But the Word of God, attested throughout thousands of years, speaks to us more clearly than all other voices. Happy are those who pay attention, who take to heart not only sweet consolation but also sharp warnings. Happy are those who feel the hand of God laid between themselves and sin, and who are then ready to lay down life and limb rather than to leave the way of salvation.

57

Wednesday Morning

The Dreadful Choice

Now the chief priests and the elders persuaded the crowd to ask for Barabbas and destroy Jesus. The governor again said to them, "Which of the two do you want me to release for you?"

They all cried out together, "Away with this man, and release to us Barabbas!"

> Matthew 27:20–21; Luke 23:18

CHRIST AND BARABBAS—what a contrast! Yet here they are put on the same level and the choice between them is left to the populace. With this act Pilate has sunk very low. He flies in the face of his statement, "I find no guilt in this man" (Luke 23:4). Yet the word of the prophecy is also fulfilled upon the Lord here: "He was numbered with the transgressors" (Isa. 53:12).

Christ rejected and Barabbas set free – what a dreadful choice! The people of God rejects its Messiah, asks for the freeing of the criminal, and so itself becomes criminal. Yet in world history Israel is not the only nation to do so. In times of war and revolution, many nations have rejected Christ and have set free and raised to power the spirit of crime and murder. What do the leaders and the demoralized masses of revolutionary parties do even today? They reject Christ, his kingdom, his commands, and his servants with the brutal cry, "Away with this man!" With their call for freedom and equality they choose Barabbas. They want to give freedom to the flesh and to set the spirit of the abyss on the throne.

Let us look into our own hearts and ask if something similar is not taking place in the inner life of many Christians. When they stray from the narrow path of the discipleship of Christ, giving rein to the flesh and its passions; when instead of working their way deeper into the living faith they flirt with the atheistic wisdom of this world and open their hearts to the doubts of the spirit of the age; when instead of overcoming their opponent by the power of truth and gentleness they fight with passionate hatred – then they too, alas, are rejecting Christ and releasing Barabbas. Happy are those who recognize this and repent before it is too late!

Christ was rejected and Barabbas set free! What disgrace and grief that meant for the Lord, and what joy for the criminal who had already been condemned to death! But this had already been decided in the plan of eternal love. The Father's compassion had willed it and the Son's surrender had accepted it. The pure and holy one was to be bound and rejected and suffer a criminal's death willingly, and in his place the guilty and condemned one was to be released from his chains and from his prison to become a son of the Father. For the name Barabbas means "Father's son."

Holy Scripture says nothing about what became of this Barabbas, but this much we know: Barabbas is representative of lost humanity (you and me) before God's judgment seat. Thus the horrible fact that Christ was rejected and Barabbas released comprises the amnesty and charter of freedom for poor sinners. Christ goes into a painful death for us, and we are absolved from guilt and punishment and raised to the liberty of the children of God. That is the deeply painful and yet glorious message of the gospel. It is the only true consolation for all poor sinners, a fountain of inexhaustible joy for all the redeemed, and the theme of eternal songs of praise.

58

Wednesday Evening

Crucify Him! Crucify Him!

Pilate said to them, "Then what shall I do with Jesus who is called Christ?" They all said, "Let him be crucified!" And he said, "Why? What evil has he done?" But they shouted all the more, "Let him be crucified!"

Matthew 27:22–23

PILATE'S PITIFUL WEAKNESS of will becomes more and more obvious. He wanted to release Jesus, for he recognized his innocence and felt the warnings of conscience. At the same time he did not want to do so, for he feared the rage of the people more than the voice of truth and right. The devil has an easy task with a weak will like this. The road to hell is paved with the good intentions of such a will.

At the cries of the crowd the procurator turns about in fear, and asks in pathetic uncertainty, "What shall I do with Jesus?" What a question! For all time there is only one right answer: believe in him, receive him into your heart, love and worship him, follow and serve him in word and deed!

We can see here in the example of the crowd the drastic power of an evil passion on the one hand, and a horrible inconstancy of mind and character on the other. Just a few days previously, they had brought their Messiah with rejoicing to the capital city. They had greeted him with jubilation and accompanied him singing, "Hosanna! Blessed is he who comes in the name of the Lord! Hosanna in the highest!" (Matt. 21:9). On Good Friday, however, the same people shouted with fanatical rage against the same King, "Crucify him! Crucify him!"

Or were they different, better people who cried, "Hosanna," and worse ones who now cried, "Crucify him"? After the enthusiasm which hailed Jesus so recently, is it possible that no one from Palm Sunday's jubilating throngs was present in front of the praetorium? The news of Jesus' capture must have spread like wildfire through the city. But there was no voice raised for the Lord, no opposing party energetically demanding his release! If the better ones stayed away or if they were waiting here in silence – as often happens in such cases – then, through their absence or silence they shared in the guilt.

After each of Pilate's questions the shouts of the people, stirred to fanaticism by the priests, grew wilder and more tumultuous. Israel had not recognized the gracious time of its visitation. It had not considered what served its peace (Luke 19: 42–44). For us, though, it is still the time of grace. Happy is the nation, happy is the house and heart that chooses Jesus as eternal King.

The Lord stood in his hidden majesty and looked down silently into the seething crowd. Deep sorrow filled his soul. He loved these people with all his saving love. He had brought them God's salvation. He had fed their hungry, comforted their wretched ones, blessed their children, healed their sick, and raised their dead. He wanted to save these people and make them holy. And they not only rejected him but demanded the death penalty – even the shameful and cruel death penalty of the Gentiles – on the accursed tree. This deed wounded his heart so that it could have bled its life away without the nails and the stab from the spear. But love did not die out in him. It drove him onward to the very cross.

Be still, my soul, when you too are deeply wounded by the ingratitude of people, their inconstancy and enmity. Be still and follow your Master.

The Man of Sorrows

Then the soldiers of the governor took Jesus into the governor's headquarters, and they gathered the whole battalion before him. And they stripped him and put a scarlet robe on him, and twisting together a crown of thorns, they put it on his head and put a reed in his right hand. And kneeling before him, they mocked him, saying, "Hail, King of the Jews!" And they spit on him and took the reed and struck him on the head.

Matthew 27:27–30

IN THE FURY AND MOCKERY of the Roman henchmen we can see to what bestiality human nature can sink when it grows hard through godlessness and gives in unreservedly to wild carnal impulses. Persecutions of Christians, the Thirty Years' War, the French Revolution, and other events in history give a shaking testimony to the same thing. What had the gentle King of truth done to those men? How had he roused their furious hate? Their insane cruelty would be incomprehensible if we did not know that behind them, unseen by humans but visible to the eyes of God, the powers of darkness were unveiling their demonic zeal. The hearts of those soldiers were inflamed, and their tongues and arms directed, by spirits of the abyss. These spirits took advantage of their hour to show what they could do and to give vent to all their hatred of God and of the Savior of the world. They were allowed to do their utmost in order that they suffer utter defeat.

We look with horror at the frenzy of hell and the fury of men, and in search of comfort and help we turn our eyes to the Man of Sorrows. There he stands, battered, crowned with thorns, covered with blood and tears. What physical pain tortures him! And still deeper is his grief of soul.

Unfathomable love had driven him to the Jews and Gentiles of this earth. He wanted to save them and gather them into one flock and as the Good Shepherd lead them to pasture on eternally green meadows. But here Jew and Gentile unite in fanatical hatred to hurl him into the abyss of disgrace and misery. He has to go through all this alone, deserted by all. No friend comes to him in his need. No one lifts a hand. No angel comforts him. Even the Father's heart seems closed to him.

He has now become the most despised and rejected one, a man of sorrows and acquainted with grief (Isa. 53:3). He bears everything in silence, patiently and submissively – only in his soul sighs: "Is there any sorrow like my sorrow? O my people, what have I done to you? How have I wearied you? Answer me" (Lam. 1:12; Mic. 6:3).

Anyone who is not moved by the grief of his Savior and by God's stern judgment has a heart of stone in his breast. For it was in our place that the Lord Jesus stood there. It was for our offenses that he suffered. With the lacerated wounds and crushing shame he had to atone for what we had earned with our sins of vanity, pride, envy, and hatred. The punishment of all humanity was poured on his head and accumulated in his heart. Nevertheless, he endured it all, not only with quiet obedience but with burning love. He knew that the salvation of lost sinners could grow only out of his deadly suffering. He knew that all who follow him in repentance, with faith and love, would go on their pilgrim way free from guilt and punishment and one day enter into his heavenly joy. Eternal thanks be to you, O Jesus!

Thursday Evening

Behold the Man!

Pilate went out again and said to them, "See, I am bringing him out to you that you may know that I find no guilt in him." So Jesus came out, wearing the crown of thorns and the purple robe. Pilate said to them, "Behold the man!"

John 19:4–5

"BEHOLD THE MAN!" Pilate called out contemptuously and with pity, without an inkling of the significance of these words. His purpose was to touch the hearts of the people and awake compassion. But in vain; they were brazenfaced and their hearts were of flint!

We condemn such hardness. Nevertheless, when the Spirit of God portrays this tortured figure before our eyes in order to touch our hearts, we often remain so dull that we ought to be appalled at our own lack of feeling. The suffering of an animal rouses our sympathy, but we pass by the suffering of our Savior with indifference. O Lord, have mercy on us and let us know and feel what you want to reveal to us here!

"Behold the man!" These words let us see our Savior in his deepest degradation and disfigurement, in the worst agonies of body and soul. The crown of suffering on his head presses deep into his holy brow the thorn that sprang from Adam's sin. The red cloak that hangs from his torn and bleeding shoulders covers him with all the shame into which man has sunk through pride and lust for power. This pitiful picture reveals to us our own earthly wretchedness. We are well pleased with ourselves. We enjoy looking at ourselves in the mirror and decking ourselves out before others, but in Christ's tortured figure we are shown ourselves as we really are. We see fallen humanity as God sees it: there is neither form nor beauty but only guilt and shame, ugliness, pain, and condemnation. We ourselves and the enemies of souls (sin, the world, and the devil) have done this to us. Yes, we have done this to him who stands there in our stead. If with this recognition we lose ourselves in contemplation of this picture of misery, then our hearts must be softened. Then we will have to weep for ourselves and our sins. We will not regret such tears, for our weeping will be turned into joy. If we recognize our own reflected image in Jesus' shame and suffering, then we will also be allowed to see our salvation in his beauty.

"Behold the man!" See the inner beauty and glory of the suffering Son of Man through the veil of outward disfigurement. There he stands in his perfect innocence and holiness, in obedience and love, in humility and majesty. The crown of thorns is his crown of honor. The cloak of mockery is his kingly purple. The drops of blood and tears are his royal diadems. That is how the Father sees him from heaven with his divine love and silently confirms in his heart, "This is my beloved Son in whom I am well pleased" (Matt. 3:17). That is how the angels who look down see him and grow speechless in adoration and worship. That is how his redeemed on earth see him. They look up to him and falling on their knees, offer him their songs of praise, "You are the fairest of the sons of men" (Ps. 45:2). In this wretched state he subdues hard hearts. In his great suffering he is the sweetest comfort and heavenly strengthening of all who are weary and heavy laden. If we have become completely his, then all that is his is also ours. The Father in heaven sees in us his beauty and glory. His image shines in our souls, his crown gleams on our heads, his royal garment is our dress of honor. The thorns on his head change the thorns of our path into fragrant roses. We are children in whom the Father is well pleased. The holy God now points to his redeemed humankind in the presence of all the angels and says with fatherly love, "Behold the man!"

Where Are You From?

*The Jews answered him, "We have a law, and according to
that law he ought to die because he has made himself the
Son of God." When Pilate heard this statement, he was even
more afraid. He entered his headquarters again and said to
Jesus, "Where are you from?" But Jesus gave him no answer.
So Pilate said to him, "You will not speak to me? Do you
not know that I have authority to release you and authority
to crucify you?" Jesus answered him, "You would have no
authority over me at all unless it had been given you from
above. Therefore he who delivered me over to you has the
greater sin."*

John 19:7–11

WHEN PILATE heard from the Jews that Jesus declared
himself to be the Son of God, a shudder went through
his soul. He remembered the heathen myths of sons of

the gods coming to this earth. He remembered that Jesus said that he was a king and that his kingdom was not of this world. He remembered his wife's warning dream. Then he was even more afraid.

It is the same with all those who hear enough about Christ to get a deep impression of him but do not believe in him. They are filled with secret fear. A prick of conscience goes with them everywhere and does not let them rest. Pilate was unhappy since he had come into such close touch with the Lord. So after he flogged him and showed him to the people, Pilate called him once more into the praetorium, thus hiding him from the sight of the Jews, and interrogated him a second time. He hoped to hear something from him that might calm his fear and asked the Lord, "Where are you from?" Once more, he had no idea of the deeper significance of his question. Christ had often answered it: to Nicodemus, to his disciples, and to the people. In his High Priestly Prayer for his disciples he had also expressed that he had come down to this poor earth from the shining heights of heaven, from the bosom of the Father. Now Pilate's frightened question may have occasioned him to lift up his eyes from this dark vale of pain to his heavenly home and so to find comfort and strength in his suffering.

Let us also consider this question. When pleasures and worries storm in upon us and we are in danger of falling into what is carnal or of losing courage in the suffering of our times – in short, when this base world seeks to enslave us – then we should take to heart the question, "Where are you from?" We should remind ourselves that we have a higher and better homeland than this poor earth, that we come from the great and glorious God, that in Christ we are born again as God's children and some day will return to the glory of heaven, to be with Christ forever. Then the things of this world will become small to us. They will not be able to hold us back in our race for the crown of life.

The Lord judged Pilate by refusing to answer this question. Instead, he merely dampened the Roman's boasting of his power by declaring, "You would have no power over me unless it had been given you from above." With this he turned away from the governor and placed himself completely in his Father's hand and power.

If only we would learn, when we are threatened and persecuted by the powers of the world, to look up in faith to him who in his own time will lay them in the dust! If only we would learn to serve him, faithfully and with courageous trust, to whom all power in heaven and on earth is given!

62

Friday Evening

The Twisted World

From then on Pilate sought to release him, but the Jews cried out, "If you release this man, you are not Caesar's friend. Everyone who makes himself a king opposes Caesar." So when Pilate heard these words, he brought Jesus out and sat down on the judgment seat at a place called The Stone Pavement, and in Aramaic Gabbatha. Now it was the day of Preparation of the Passover. It was about the sixth hour. He said to the Jews, "Behold your King!" They cried out, "Away with him, away with him, crucify him!" Pilate said to them, "Shall I crucify your King?" The chief priests answered, "We have no king but Caesar." So he delivered him over to them to be crucified.

John 19:12–15

WHERE THE DEVIL REIGNS, everything becomes twisted: Pilate the friend of Caesar, the Jews Roman patriots, Christ a rebel deserving death!

Pilate the friend of Caesar! The governor did not have a vicious nature. He was not devoid of feeling, for Jesus made an impression on him and he felt pity for his distress. He was also not without a conscience, for he opposed the sentence of death vigorously. Christ himself judged him mildly when he said, "He who delivered me to you has the greater sin." The situation in which he found himself was a very difficult one, and thousands of so-called good people in his place would have done as he did. Tiberius, the Roman emperor at that time, was a suspicious, bloodthirsty tyrant. It was to his favor that Pilate owed his high office, and now while he was making a final effort to set Jesus free, the fanatical people threatened to accuse him to the emperor. They accused him of siding with a rebel and shouted, "If you release this man, you are not Caesar's friend!" At that the judge grew pale: his office, health, and happiness – his life – was at stake. One word from the emperor and he would be thrown into prison or put to death. Of course, it is just such a sacrifice of self that Christ requires of all who want to become his disciples. That was too much for Pilate to bear.

Pilate, however, still had to pay a price. In order to remain the emperor's friend he breaks the emperor's law. In order to remain a judge he tramples justice under foot. To remain a statesman he undermines the foundations of the state. Woe to rulers who have friends and servants like this! Woe to officials who for the favor of their employers reject Christ! The world's friendship is enmity to God.

The Jews Roman patriots! If Pilate really set Christ free, then the chief priests would lose everything. Then the maltreated One could again preach in public and perform miracles. There was no doubt that then the mood of the people would change completely. That would be the end of their power and reputation forever. Then it would be they who were rejected and trampled upon by the people. So they restrained their hatred of the Roman yoke, hypocritically wrapped the cloak of Roman patriotism about them, and shouted, "We have no king but Caesar!" Thus they rejected their Messiah, their Liberator, and made themselves slaves to worldly power. This is not an isolated case of such political hypocrisy. It has often been repeated in history, but it has always estranged the wretched hypocrites from the King of Truth and enchained them in the fetters of the hated tyrants.

Christ a rebel deserving death! All guilt was heaped upon the Holy One, who was not only obedient unto death himself but had constantly admonished his own to be obedient to God and to the earthly government. Should his disciples then be surprised if they fare like their Master: if they are executed as godless men and branded as rebels (or at least banished as disturbers of the peace as soon as they refuse to worship the gods of this world)? But even in this twisted world the Lord kept his spotless purity and his eternal kingdom through silence and endurance. Follow him, all who want to be his subjects.

63

Saturday Morning

Pilate Washes His Hands

So when Pilate saw that he was gaining nothing, but rather that a riot was beginning, he took water and washed his hands before the crowd, saying, "I am innocent of this righteous man's blood; see to it yourselves."

Matthew 27:24

PILATE FELT that a terrible bloodguilt lay upon his conscience. As he did not want to carry this guilt, he performed a symbolic act. He had a basin of water brought to him and washed his hands in the sight of the crowd. He believed that with this act he could stand before the people and his own conscience guiltless of this judicial murder. So he testified once more to Jesus' righteousness and pushed all the blame from himself onto the people, saying, "I am innocent of this righteous man's blood; see to it yourselves!"

But his efforts were in vain. The reproach that it was he who sacrificed this righteous man continued to burn within him, and throughout all the centuries he has remained branded in the eyes of the whole world as the unjust judge. Yet he was right in feeling that a person can have peace only if, in all circumstances and struggles, he keeps his hands clean – that is, a clear conscience. Everyone of moral character knows this. That is why David prayed so ardently, "Create in me a clean heart, O God!" (Ps. 51:10). That is why Christ himself testified so impressively, "Blessed are the pure in heart, for they shall see God" (Matt. 5:8). Accordingly, innumerable Christians have striven for purification of conscience. Many of them, however, are so foolish as to imagine that like Pilate they can achieve the purification of their inner lives by outward actions. Such things as fasting, almsgiving, attending church, outwardly observing the Lord's Supper, and castigating the body are supposed to make a person pleasing to God and satisfied with himself. Vain effort, ill-fated torment! Seriously thinking people will be driven to despair, while the thoughtless succumb completely to the pleasures of the world.

The only way of salvation is and remains the narrow path of repentance, faith, and consecration. Whoever wants to have a pure heart must recognize his own guilt and stop trying to push it onto the shoulders of others. Are we free of guilt for Christ's crucifixion? Do we want to push it all onto Pilate and the Jews? Oh, no! The cry comes to us too from the soul of our suffering Savior, "You have burdened me with your sins, you have wearied me with your iniquities" (Isa. 43:24). The blessing of Christ's cross will begin for us only at the moment when we admit with bleeding hearts that it is we who put him to death. But with repentance must come the living faith that confesses with certainty, "I believe in the forgiveness of my sins." Herein lies the strength to fight sin and do our best to follow Christ in deed and truth. Every morning and every evening we have to crucify our old nature so that the new nature in us may rise daily with Christ to the blessed life of Easter day. Then we will begin to experience in ourselves the immeasurable depth and glory of the words, "Blessed are the pure in heart, for they shall see God."

64

Saturday Evening

Christ's Blood as Curse
and as Blessing

And all the people answered, "His blood be on us and on our children!"

So Pilate decided that their demand should be granted. He released the man who had been thrown into prison for insurrection and murder, for whom they asked, but he delivered Jesus over to their will.

Matthew 27:25; Luke 23:24–25

WHEREAS PILATE tried vainly to rid himself of the guilt for Jesus' death, the people eagerly took it upon themselves with, crying, "His blood be on us and on our children!" Those are terrible words, calling a curse upon themselves. When Cain killed his brother Abel, the Lord said to him, "The voice of your brother's blood is crying to me from the ground" (Gen. 4:10). It cried to heaven for retribution and revenge. How much more powerfully, how much more effectively, does the blood of Christ, the firstborn of all brothers, cry against his murderers to the heart of the Father on high. A curse came upon that nation. It came upon them and their children in the dreadful destruction of Jerusalem, in the bloody slaughter of countless sons and daughters of Israel, in the cruel slavery of the survivors, in the dispersion of the whole nation among the peoples of the earth. In spite of this, the nation did not die. They are still a people, though they have no temple.

The blood of Christ, the Son of God, has also come upon us, upon the people of the new covenant – but praise God, not as a curse but as a blessing. There have been trends within the church in which Christ's blood and wounds were treated in a fanciful, soft manner with songs and tears. The subject is too serious for that. With grateful adoration we surrender ourselves in faith to the mystery of the redemption, to the blessing of the blood of Christ. But this blood also calls from earth to heaven. It speaks of the unending grief of our Savior, of how he trembled and flinched, of the cutting blows of the lash and of the sharp spines of the crown of thorns. It speaks of his pierced hands and feet and of the whole agony of his death on the accursed tree. But it also testifies to the divine love that is greater than all the torture of the cross. It cries to heaven with a voice that breaks the Father's heart and overwhelms us: "Grace! Grace! Grace for lost sinners!" Grace for you and me, for the blood of the Son of God cleanses us from all sin – and even though they were red as blood, they are to become white as snow. It washes clean all who are repentant and fills the believing with new life. Life is in the blood (Lev. 17:14). In the blood of Christ his life is imparted to us. In the Lord's Supper it quenches the thirst of the thirsty and fills them with the powers of the heavenly life and of blessed resurrection. Christ's blood and righteousness is our dress of honor, and all who have made their clothing bright in the blood of the Lamb shall enter into heaven's eternal joy.

Fifth Week of Lent

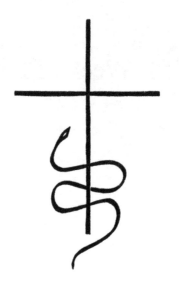

65

Sunday Morning

He Bore His Cross

Then he delivered him over to be crucified. So they took
Jesus, and he went out, bearing his own cross.

John 19:16–17

PILATE'S LAST EFFORT to save Jesus was crushed by
the threat, "If you release this man, you are not Caesar's
friend!" So he delivered the Holy One to his executioners to be crucified, and the Lord began his painful walk
to Golgotha.

"He bore his own cross." In these simple words
the Gospel reports the Lord's great deed of love. He
had already borne many burdens, but none had been
as heavy as this cross. He was completely exhausted
after his inner struggle in Gethsemane, the physical
and spiritual abuse of that night of horror, the bloody
flogging in the praetorium, and the prospect of a cruel
death. Now he had to load the heavy beam of the cross

upon his wounded shoulder. Shattered, his face pallid, his head crowned with thorns, he walked between two criminals, accompanied by gaping and mocking crowds. That would be enough to make anyone else succumb who felt as deeply as he – but he bore his cross. Yet in this cross there was more to be borne than human eyes could see or the mind could grasp. There were burdens that he alone could comprehend: the sins of all sinners, the suffering of all humanity, the terrible judgment of God's wrath. That was the immense weight that made this cross so heavy. And yet – he bore his cross. We look at him and say in adoration, "Behold the Lamb of God, who bears the sin of the world!" (John 1:29).

For he carried his cross for us – also for you and me. Now, when he lays a cross upon his disciples, they have only the smallest part of it to carry. The real burden, the curse of sin, he took upon himself alone. So our cross is essentially an admonition to repentance, a school of patience, a means toward the strengthening of our faith. Indeed, it should become for us a badge of honor, testifying that we are accounted worthy to enter the Lord's holy order of the cross, and united with him to gain the crown through suffering.

66

Sunday Evening

Simon of Cyrene

And as they led him away, they seized one Simon of Cyrene, who was coming in from the country, and laid on him the cross, to carry it behind Jesus.

Luke 23:26

THE LORD BORE HIS CROSS in unflinching obedience, gentle patience, and faithful love. But the burden was so heavy that his strength threatened to give way under it. When the soldiers saw how he staggered they feared that the whole procession might be held up by his collapse. So they roughly laid hold of a man who was just coming from his fields, and compelled him to help the Lord carry his cross. He resisted, to be sure. He did not want to do it, but he had to.

To begin with, he probably bent under the load with grim, concealed rage. As his feelings calmed down on this way to the crucifixion, however, and as he saw more deeply into the eyes and heart of the holy Sufferer, doubtless a wonderful peace came over him. Probably it was then that the first rays of eternal salvation shone into his soul. Then he was ready to bear the cross, not only because he had to, but because he wanted to.

Indeed, he surely regarded it afterwards as a great and undeserved grace and honor to have been accounted worthy to help his Savior in his very great need. We may draw the conclusion that his bearing of the cross brought him eternal blessing from the fact that he is referred to as the father of Alexander and Rufus, two well-known members of the early church (see Rom. 16:13). Wherever the Lord's cross is preached, the story of Simon is told, as is that of Mary's anointing. More significantly, he is now forever with his Lord in the heavenly paradise.

If such a thing were possible in Christ's kingdom, believers could envy him the blows and mocking words with which he was compelled to become the sole comrade of his eternal King in the midst of his enemies. Yet the same thing has fallen to the share of all martyrs. Indeed, there are nameless millions who bear a cross for the Lord in silence. They probably also resisted at first and wished only to be relieved of their cross. But, since looking more deeply into their

Master's face and realizing that they are bearing one cross with him, they have become quiet. They see that through their cross they are being renewed, consecrated, and transfigured to be like him. They see too that when they are about to collapse he sends them a helpful Simon at the decisive moment. So in spite of all that they have to bear, they rejoice that their names are written in heaven (Luke 10:20).

The Lord (who knows as no other the bitterness of suffering and how hard it is to bear the cross) now spreads out his arms of love to all his cross-bearers and says to them, "Come to me, all who labor and are heavy laden, and I will give you rest. Take my yoke upon you and learn from me, for I am gentle and lowly in heart, and you will find rest for your souls. For my yoke is easy, and my burden is light" (Matt. 11:28–30).

67

Monday Morning

The Weeping Daughters of Jerusalem

And there followed him a great multitude of the people and of women who were mourning and lamenting for him.

Luke 23:27

WHEREAS MANY CROSS-BEARERS may today strive towards the eternal goal quietly and unobserved, the Lord was followed on his road to the crucifixion by a great multitude of people. They were the crowds whose cry, "Crucify him! Crucify him! His blood be on us and on our children!" probably still sounded in his ears. They wanted to enjoy the triumph of their evil deed and accompany their victim with scornful looks and words.

Such great suffering calmly borne, however, usually finds sympathy somewhere, and here in the crowd there were daughters of Jerusalem who had tender hearts.

"They mourned and lamented for him." Some preachers have suggested that their tears made little difference. It is true that Christianity does not consist merely of tender feelings; it is deed and life. Tears without change are worthless. Tears that come from superficial emotion are dried by the next breath of wind. Some people are able to weep bitterly below Christ's cross and a few moments later laugh in the enjoyment of worldly pleasure. The worst thing is that people often deceive themselves with such tears. They imagine that they are very devout because of these tears, but their hearts are not changed. Their manner of life belies their tears. Let us be on our guard against such self-deception!

Nevertheless, we are glad to know that among the wicked people who accompanied the Lord to his death there were at least some souls whose tears showed natural human sympathy. Let us not forget that worse than the superficial tears of the easily moved is the immense indifference to God and to the suffering and death of the Lord Jesus which has settled on many hearts like a mountain.

We have to ask: Don't these daughters of Jerusalem put us to shame? We are Christians and understand the significance of the Lord's cross, yet hasn't an awful insensitivity to the Lord also come over us? Aren't there many among us who have compassion for people and animals but care little about the Lord's cross? They have not even a tear for the great Man of Sorrows, this heart of compassionate love that shed its blood in the agony of death for us. Doesn't this indifference make us uneasy? Don't we feel uneasy when we consider that the tears of those women will witness against us on the great day of reckoning? The Lord himself, who had no answer for Herod and Pilate, did so far recognize the tears of those women as to count them worthy of a serious and noble answer.

68

Monday Evening

The Lord's Last Call
to Repentance

But turning to them Jesus said, "Daughters of Jerusalem, do not weep for me, but weep for yourselves and for your children. For behold, the days are coming when they will say, 'Blessed are the barren and the wombs that never bore and the breasts that never nursed!' Then they will begin to say to the mountains, 'Fall on us,' and to the hills, 'Cover us.' For if they do these things when the wood is green, what will happen when it is dry?"

Luke 23:28–31

THE CROSS-BEARING REDEEMER had veiled himself in deep silence on the first part of his sorrowful road, but when he became aware of the tears of the women accompanying him, he lifted himself out of it and turned his thorn-crowned head to the daughters of Jerusalem. The condemned man has now become

231

a prophet. Powerful words proceed from his mouth, proving that he has not broken down under the cross, but that he has preserved his eternal majesty. "Do not weep for me!" By that he means, "I do not need your pity. The cross will become my scepter and the crown of thorns my glory. It is true that I am dying, but I shall rise again. I am condemned, but I shall come again to judge the world. Weep for yourselves and for your children."

With this last call to repentance, the Lord knocks once more at the hearts of Zion's children. Before his prophetic range of vision the future of Jerusalem is unrolled. He sees the fall of the royal city, the walls razed to the ground, the temple burning. He hears the furious clamor of the victorious enemies and the despairing lament of the conquered and crushed.

He wants to direct the minds of those accompanying him to the terrible might of the approaching divine judgment. "If this is done to me, the green wood, the tree of life, how you – branches cut off from the tree of life and withered in sin – will burn in the fire of God's judgment!" But the Lord does not say this as a threat, but in order to save. Here too he bears in mind that he has come to seek and to save the lost (Luke 19:10). He points out to them the only way that can still save them before the day of wrath dawns. This way consists of tears – not tears of weak pity for our own suffering or for that of others, but tears of holy repentance. That is the way of salvation for Jerusalem's children and also for us.

Fellow Christians, do you know these tears? Have you learned to weep for yourself and for your sins? Such tears are essential but not as though they were a merit that will buy heaven. (Was Peter thinking of gaining something when he went out and wept bitterly?) They alone open our heart to the Savior. They alone melt the ice of our old nature, and under them alone a new heavenly life comes into bloom. So weep for your cold, weak hearts. Weep that you have not yet grown better in spite of your Savior's indescribable work of love. Weep for your sins! You young men who have sworn loyalty to the Lord, such tears as Peter's tears do not disgrace you. You older men, who have grown firm in the storms of life and regard it as a matter of honor to suppress pain and master all emotionalism, these tears do not disgrace you. They spring from a divine sorrow and yield the fruit of peace and righteousness in all who shed them. And you womanly souls, let your tears have free course – not as a sign of fleeting emotion but of a deep repentance.

69

Tuesday Morning

Golgotha

And they brought him to the place called Golgotha (which means Place of a Skull).

Mark 15:22

JERUSALEM WAS SURROUNDED on three sides by deep ravines. Only to the north did the landscape stretch out more evenly. Here, close to the city wall, some wealthy families had built country houses in which to spend the summer and had planted pleasure gardens. From their flat roofs they had a fine view of the royal city with its gleaming golden temple and proud palaces, and toward the east, the Mount of Olives with its olive and palm groves. But bordering on those pleasure gardens, close to the military road, there was a sad and desolate spot. It was the little hill Golgotha, the place of a skull. Here the lowest and meanest of humankind, criminals condemned to be put to death by crucifixion, were executed. A passerby felt a shudder go through him when he hurried by the accursed place.

This spot was the end of the Via Dolorosa, the Lord's way of suffering. Here he and two evildoers, surrounded by large and mixed throngs, were brought from the praetorium by the soldiers and executioners. We too have accompanied our Savior thus far. With him we have reached Golgotha. Let us stand here quietly and reflect upon the immense significance of this place.

No matter where our pilgrimage takes us, the end is always a place of a skull. No matter what ages our minds pass through, nowhere do our hearts, full of sin and longing, find true peace and new life except in what was now about to take place at Golgotha.

The shining peaks of the Alps are beautiful; the jagged rocks of Sinai are holy; it is good to be on the Mount of Transfiguration. But all these proud heights are far surpassed in importance by the little hill Golgotha. Here is the turning point of all ages. This is the place of the greatest pain, of death, and of the curse, but at the same time it is the place of the greatest, most glorious, and most blessed revelation of God's love in Christ. Here is the spring from which the stream of grace flows as eternal blessing over the whole world. This is the place of refuge for the erring and the lost, for those who labor and are heavy laden; the place where the wounded and hard-pressed fighter finds peace. Here the old man dies, and here the new man is born for eternal life.

A grand vista is opened up for us at this spot, Golgotha. Behind us lies the lost paradise, and from where we stand we lift our eyes to the hills whence our help comes (Ps. 121:1). Before us we can see the golden turrets of the heavenly Jerusalem.

70

Tuesday Evening

The Cross

There they crucified him . . .
John 19:18

WITH THE HELP of Simon of Cyrene the Lord had carried his heavy cross to Golgotha. Then it was set up and firmly implanted in the ground by the henchmen. In silence the exhausted, thorn-crowned Savior stood, watching their work. He remembered the prophecies of his suffering and death and saw in the cross the altar on which atonement was now to be made for the redemption of the world.

We, too, look at the Lord's cross at this hour and consider in quiet worship what it has to say to us. There it stands on Golgotha, and its dark form towers above the world, above all ages. It speaks to us of sin and pain, of death and damnation. It shows us how wicked the human race is in God's eyes, for in increasing disobedience it feeds on the forbidden fruit of the tree of destruction. The cross is the tree of the curse and of death, but it also testifies powerfully to the transforming power of God's love and mercy.

Since Christ bore the cross and since it bore him, it has become to the Lord himself the sign of his glory, of his victory and lordship, as the prophecy says, "The government shall be upon his shoulder" (Isa. 9:6). The cross is the scepter with which he rules the world, the sword with which he overcomes his enemies. It is the shepherd's staff with which he leads his flock to pasture on the eternally green meadows of his grace. For the lost world, the cross is now the altar of reconciliation, where it finds forgiveness and peace. For the redeemed children of God it has become the tree of life. Its fruits win for them healing from all wounds and sickness, and the eternal joy of paradise. As a banner of salvation it lights the way for all nations.

The foot of the cross that sinks into the earth says urgently to us, "From the dust you were taken, and to dust you shall return" (Gen. 3:19). "Set your house in order, for you must die" (2 Kings 20:1). Conquer death while you are alive.

The two arms which are stretched out over the earth call to us, "The earth is yours. The redeemed are all your brothers and sisters. Embrace, bear, and comfort them with the love of Christ. Love as long as you are able to love!"

The head of the cross lifted up to heaven says to your soul, "Seek the things that are above where Christ is at the right hand of the Father" (Col. 3:1). It shows you the wonderful goal of your pilgrimage, your eternal home. All the sorrow and suffering that a Christian still has to bear in this earthly life changes for him henceforth into a blessed cross.

71

Wednesday Morning

The Crucifixion

*And they offered him wine mixed with myrrh, but he did
not take it.*

Mark 15:23

THE PROCEEDINGS before Pilate had taken place
early on Good Friday morning. It might have been
about nine in the morning when the escort with the
three condemned men reached Golgotha in the hot
spring sunshine. The work necessary for the execution
was quickly undertaken and the three crosses erected.

Crucifixion was the Romans' most cruel and igno-
minious means of execution. It meant that the criminal
was not worthy to touch the earth with his feet and
that his elevated head was given to the vengeance
of the gods. The Lord let this terrible form of capital
punishment be carried out upon him. But first the
condemned men were offered wine mixed with myrrh,

a numbing drink to lessen their torment. The Lord refused it, however, for he wanted to be fully conscious as he drank his Father's cup. Not a drop was to be taken unperceptively.

Then the dreadful sentence was carried out.

Now he hangs on the accursed tree, an outcast between heaven and earth. His pale face is bent forward. His arms that opened lovingly to the weary and heavy-laden are drawn taut against the crossbeam. His hands that healed the sick and blessed little children are fastened to it with iron nails, and his feet, which had walked the path to salvation, are bored through and securely nailed to the lower end of the cross. His holy blood, flowing from the burning wounds, runs down into the sand of Golgotha and blesses the earth that has rejected him.

What pains shoot through his quivering body and what thoughts and feelings pass through his holy soul! No one can fathom his sorrow that all his loving efforts for the welfare of his people have to end like this. No one at the time could conceive that all the misery of the whole of lost humanity was concentrated in this one heart. He alone knew and felt it all, and he alone pondered the immense guilt that the human race brought upon itself with this blackest of all crimes.

But he saw still deeper. He saw that his murderers were just unhappy tools of an invisible power: he saw how the kingdom of darkness stormed upon him, rousing his human enemies and fighting desperately to gain victory.

His pain was heightened by the fact that the devil was permitted to triumph mockingly over him and to ensnare Jews and Gentiles in his power. Jesus alone was fully conscious that his suffering was atoning suffering: that the Father's eternal plan of love should be fulfilled through his crucifixion and that in his excruciating death the salvation of the lost world would be brought about. He knew that with his last breath a tremendous change must take place: the fall of the prince of this world, the beginning of the glad tidings of peace, and the fulfillment of his own prophecy, "When I am lifted up from the earth, I will draw all people to myself" (John 12:32).

As for us, we fall on our knees, cover our faces, and worship the love that surpasses all thought.

72

Wednesday Evening

Accounted a Criminal

And with him they crucified two robbers, one on his right
and one on his left. And the Scripture was fulfilled that says,
"He was numbered with the transgressors."

Mark 15:27–28

"THE HOUR IS COMING when you will leave me alone,"
the Lord said at his farewell meal with his disciples
(John 16:32). This time of his loneliness came all too
soon. We can imagine how hard that was for him, since
we are born for fellowship, and only in fellowship can
we feel joy and happiness. But people who are misun-
derstood by their loved ones in fulfilling a higher task,
who are constantly opposed by those around them, feel
especially lonely.

What task could be compared to that of the Savior
of the world? What forsakenness could be compared

to his? He was alone in Gethsemane where he wrestled with death while his disciples slept. He was alone when he was arrested and led away while his disciples fled. He stood alone before the Sanhedrin, before Herod, and before Pilate. He stood alone under the lash of his executioners, and alone he hung dying on the cross. For even the few faithful souls who were close to him there did not understand him and his suffering and could neither comfort nor help him. What pain that must have been to his loving heart!

Yet he was given company on his last road and at Golgotha: two common criminals were brought out with him and crucified, one on his right and one on his left. In this way the prophecy was fulfilled, that he was to be numbered with the transgressors (Isa. 53:12).

Any decent man would have regarded it as deep humiliation to have to sit with such evildoers even in some secluded corner. He would find the disgrace unbearable to be considered one of them in public and treated like them. And Jesus, the pure and exalted one, was not only regarded as one of this murderous gang but was slandered as their leader.

Jesus, however, made no objection to this. He did not consider the disgrace, nor did he reject this company. Indeed he spoke words of love to one of these thieves.

He himself came down to evildoers. He wanted to be regarded as one of them and to take their curse upon himself. This will become our greatest comfort as soon as we realize that in God's sight we so-called respectable people are evildoers on whom the sentence of condemnation has already been passed, and who with every step are drawing nearer to death and judgment.

How comforting it is to have the Lord accompany us! For by becoming one of us and taking our disgrace upon himself, he frees us from the evil enemy and brings us into community with himself and his angels. Thus he makes us living members of the heavenly family.

Now it is important for us to avoid all destructive relationships and yet to treat the evildoers whom we meet with kindness. Most of all, we must strive with all our powers to live and walk in personal fellowship with our still invisible Savior until we see him face to face.

73

Thursday Morning

The Gathering of the Nations

Pilate also wrote an inscription, and put it on the cross. It read, 'Jesus of Nazareth, the King of the Jews'. Many of the Jews read this inscription, for the place where Jesus was crucified was near the city, and it was written in Aramaic, in Latin, and in Greek. So the chief priests of the Jews said to Pilate, "Do not write, 'The King of the Jews', but rather, 'This man said, I am King of the Jews'." Pilate answered, "What I have written I have written."

John 19:19–22

PILATE HAD SUFFERED a heavy defeat. He had allowed himself to be compelled by the Jews against both law and conscience to condemn to death one who was innocent. He tried to take his revenge by means of biting satire, by the inscription on Christ's cross: "Jesus of Nazareth, the King of the Jews." This taunt infuriated the Jews who demanded that the inscription be changed.

But in this instance the usually fickle and inconstant governor remained firm. He answered, "What I have written I have written." In this too, though he was not aware of it, he was a servant of divine providence, for with his inscription he made a grand statement and bore witness powerfully to truth. In accordance with God's plan, this title was to remain as it was written, never to be erased by the opposition but to shine out through all times and into eternity. It was written in the three most universal languages of that time and place, and most who went by could read it.

The building of the tower of Babel had split the human race into many nationalities. These forgot their common origin, formed isolated hostile groups, and tore each other up in bloody civil wars. Thus they destroyed the morals and well-being of the whole human race. But what was dispersed by the building of that tower shall now come together again and unite in brotherly love under the cross on Golgotha. That indelible inscription contains the core of the whole gospel. Now it is written and read in numerous languages, and through the work of mission it calls and gathers all nations of the world into the one great kingdom of the eternal King.

At present the constant hostilities of the nations with their wars and instruments of murder and mass slaughter testify that the spirit of the gospel has not yet pervaded the life of the peoples. The spirit of heathendom has remained in power.

But where deep, complete conversion has taken place and pardoned sinners have really surrendered to the Crucified One, barriers fall, enmity disappears, and people are bound together as brothers and sisters. Peace appears, love rules, and Christ's kingdom is established. The prophecy of a glorious future is contained in what has taken place so far only in small circles, mostly unseen by the eyes of the world. When the Lord Christ destroys the antichrist and his gospel wins complete victory, then all the nations will be united under the banner of the eternal King. In his great kingdom of peace they will experience the blessed fulfillment of the promise, "There will be one flock and one shepherd" (John 10:16).

74

Thursday Evening

The Inscription on the Cross

"Jesus of Nazareth, the King of the Jews."
John 19:19

THE INSCRIPTION ON THE CROSS was "Jesus of Nazareth, the King of the Jews." It was written in three languages and designated the name, origin, office, and sphere of jurisdiction of the Crucified One. How much was contained in one brief phrase!

The name is Jesus and is the name above all names, for Jesus means God's salvation, the savior, the one who makes blessed. The angel had told Joseph, "You shall call his name Jesus, for he will save his people from their sins" (Matt. 1:21). He has brought God's salvation to us as well. He wants to save us too and lead us, as the true Joshua, into the heavenly Canaan. "There is salvation in no one else, for there is no other name under heaven given among men by which we must be saved" (Acts

4:12). So that must remain for us the most precious and most holy of all names.

"Of Nazareth" tells his origin. Actually he was born in Bethlehem, and the scribes would have done well to research his birthplace more exactly, which had been foretold by the prophet Micah. But Nazareth was the home of his childhood and youth, and so this small and despised village in Galilee became world-famous. It will never be forgotten, even when all the magnificent palaces in the world have become rubble. Happy the house and happy the village where Jesus found his home. Here we can also remember the related word, "Nazarite" ("One consecrated to God"), for as one consecrated to God, the Lord accomplished his work and suffered his sacrificial death.

The word "King" tells us his office. It was as king that the prophets foretold him, as king that the wise men from the east worshipped him, and as king that he was hailed by the jubilant crowds on Palm Sunday. He testified before Pilate that he was a king, and as king he hung upon the cross. In the dark hours of his death struggle he probably felt nothing of royal glory. Poor and naked, forsaken and mocked, he hung on the accursed tree. But we know that the cross has become his throne and the crown of thorns his diadem. Living and dying, he is the King of Glory in accordance with God's plan, and he will be king forever, raised to God's right hand. He consecrates his redeemed as kings and priests on earth. In the humbleness and grief of their pilgrimage, they likewise feel little or nothing of this glory; but when their Lord appears in his majesty, they too, with all the angels and heavenly hosts, will wear the crown of life with joy (Rev. 2:10).

The additional phrase "of the Jews" tells us his immediate sphere of influence. As the Son of David, as the Messiah sent by God, he is Israel's King. It is true, the Jews rejected him and the heathen jeered at their messianic hope. But the Lord remains the eternal Messiah, and through his death he has spread his rule over all other nations as well. For he died for all. He dearly bought them all and made them citizens of his kingdom. All who obey him in faith and love are now his pardoned subjects. All who reject him are rebels. But they remain under his authority and must one day kneel before him.

At the same time, as the Son of God, he is the King of all worlds. He himself bears witness, "All authority in heaven and on earth has been given to me" (Matt. 28:18). Consequently he rules in the realm of nature as he does in the realm of grace and will one day rule in the realm of glory. His kingdom has no end and his scepter is everlasting. Blessed are all who serve him with joy and continue steadfastly praying, "Thy kingdom come!"

75

Friday Morning

The First Word from the Cross

And it was the third hour, when they crucified him.

And Jesus said, "Father, forgive them, for they know not what they do."

Mark 15:25; Luke 23:34

THE LORD'S CRUCIFIXION was carried out at nine o'clock in the morning of Good Friday. He had not uttered a word since calling the daughters of Jerusalem to repentance, and even during the cruel act of crucifixion he had remained in deep silence. It was only when it was done that he opened his pale lips and cried, "Father, forgive them, for they know not what they do."

These words reveal his heart to us and the thoughts that fill his holy soul while in dying torment. He is not angry. He neither threatens nor complains. Painfully but at peace, he cries, "Father!" Thus even in death he testifies that he is the Son of God, that his conscience is clear, and that now as always he shares in the closest fellowship of love with his Father. Hatred and mockery play their grisly game below the cross, but on the cross above them the breath of heaven, the spirit of prayer, holds sway. Here the Crucified One shows us the way to the Father's heart, the way that we too must take when we are in distress and dying. But he does more than show us the way; he opens its portal to us through his bloody sacrifice.

In a like situation others might have cursed their murderers or cried out for help and mercy. Christ overcomes his own pain. He sees the tremendous bloodguilt of his murderers and the darkness that fills them. He sees the clouds of judgment piling up above them and the earth opening to swallow them all. Filled with compassion, he prays for his wretched enemies, "Father, forgive them!"

He is the only one who can save them. He takes all the horror of the judgment into the depths of his soul, comes into his Father's presence adorned with his holy wounds, and pleads and gains forgiveness for his enemies. Thus he hides the godless from the lightning of the Almighty with the shield of his intercession.

What love and compassion, what power and majesty are in this prayer of the Crucified One! He has procured help and deliverance for all humanity. He has obtained forgiveness of sins for the whole world. He has become the Savior who brings blessing to lost sinners.

Now, if his intercession is to become our salvation, two things are necessary. We must first realize that we share the guilt of his murderers. It must cut us to the marrow that we have brought him to the cross: our pride crowned him with thorns; our fleshly lust lashed his back; our evil deeds nailed his hands and feet. We put him to death.

Then, we must believe with our whole soul in the forgiveness of sins, in the power of Christ's intercession and of his vicarious death for us. When old offenses rise up in our consciences and try to accuse and torment us, when new guilt makes the old burden still heavier and we are ready to despair, then one thing alone can give us comfort and peace: the living trust that "I too have been baptized into his death. He has washed me clean with his blood. He has included me and pardoned me in his prayer, 'Father, forgive them!'"

76

Friday Evening

They Know Not What They Do

"Father, forgive them, for they know not what they do."
Luke 23:34

IN THE CRUCIFIED ONE'S PRAYER for his enemies, he modified their guilt before his Father by saying with amazing gentleness, "They know not what they do." How comforting for all sinners is this merciful verdict by him who one day will judge the world! He knows what wretched creatures we are; he remembers that we are dust. The cruel soldiers certainly did not know what they were doing. Pilate knew more, the Jewish people still more, and the Sanhedrin most of all. The people knew not only that he was innocent but that he was a great prophet and had done great deeds. The fact that the whole population rejected him and so passionately supported his crucifixion is a baffling mystery. The gospel, however, explains it, for it tells that the chief priests had delivered him up out of envy.

It always irritates envious people to meet someone great who stands out more than them. They cannot bear to be reminded of their own pettiness by the presence of such a person. This was the case of the leaders of Israel. In addition, they not only feared losing their influence on the people through the Lord's growing power but were enraged and embittered by his merciless exposure of their self-righteousness and hypocrisy. So their envy turned into deadly hatred, which blinded their minds, and then could not rest until nobleness was overthrown and meanness had come once more to power.

That was the attitude of the leaders; but how was it possible that they succeeded in changing the crowd so suddenly? The people had experienced nothing but good from the Lord. They had followed him with enthusiasm and only five days earlier had hailed him jubilantly as their Messiah. Were the cries of rage on Good Friday due only to incitement by the leaders? No, the source of the people's guilt lay deeper: in their aversion to repentance and change of heart; and in the unbelief and worldliness of their hearts.

It had been so for centuries. That was why the prophets had foretold the tragic fate of the coming Messiah, and why from the beginning of his ministry the Lord himself foresaw his painful death. The crime of Good Friday was not simply a matter of hastiness; it was the dreadful end of a long-prepared, destructive line of development. To be sure, the people did not want to kill their Messiah, but they gave in to the delusion that Jesus was an impostor and was misleading them. Because of this the mystery of his nature was hidden from them and, however guilty they were in their ignorance, they did not know that they were bringing the Lord of Glory to the cross. They had no idea that here at Golgotha the decisive battle between the kingdom of light and the kingdom of darkness was being fought – much less that they themselves were instruments in the hand of Satan. That is why the Lord prayed for them and said with deep compassion, "They know not what they do."

May we learn to judge all evildoers and our enemies as kindly as the Lord Christ does! May we learn to forgive sincerely those who insult and persecute us personally and pray to God for their forgiveness! What peace there would then be in the church of Christ and what joyous fellowship would then flourish in her!

77

Saturday Morning

Lots Cast for His Clothes

When the soldiers had crucified Jesus, they took his garments and divided them into four parts, one part for each soldier; also his tunic. But the tunic was seamless, woven in one piece from top to bottom, so they said to one another, "Let us not tear it, but cast lots for it to see whose it shall be." This was to fulfill the Scripture which says, "They divided my garments among them, and for my clothing they cast lots."

John 19:23–24

THOUSANDS OF YEARS BEFOREHAND the psalmist prophesied that lots would be cast for the Lord's clothing: "They divide my garments among them, and for my clothing they cast lots" (Ps. 22:18).

Into what deep poverty and nakedness the Lord had to sink! The birds have their nests and the foxes their holes, but the Son of Man had no place of his own on earth where he could lay his head (Matt. 8:20). Today we try as far as is possible to care for, comfort, and refresh even the poorest among us who are dying. But the dying Lord had no quiet room, no comfortable bed, and no loving hand to wipe the sweat from his brow. Even his last belongings, his clothes, were taken from him. Nailed to the rough shaft of the cross, he had to hang naked in the burning heat of the sun under the open sky, and lay his weary head down upon his own breast. But by giving up everything he had – his life – he paid our debts and made us rich through his poverty. He earned for us food and clothing and all that we need for body and soul so that we may sing, "The Lord is my shepherd, I shall not want" (Ps. 23:1).

In times of happiness, when we enjoy all the rich benefits of our God, and even in times of sickness when we are cared for by others, let us remember with tears of gratitude that the Lord Jesus earned all this for us through his deprivations and suffering. If we ourselves are tested by want and hard circumstances, let us lift up our eyes to the Crucified One. In comparison with him we are still rich. Let us understand that it is an honor to become like him and strive for the poverty of which the Lord himself said, "Blessed are the poor in spirit, for theirs is the kingdom of heaven" (Matt. 5:3). We have to consider the precious seamless and indivisible garment of his innocence and holiness as our true treasure and put it on daily. He wove it for us with his great pain and deep wretchedness. When we are adorned in this garment, our miserable pride in wealth and vanity in dress will disappear like mist before the sun, and we shall be rich and joyful in God even in times of deprivation.

The Mocking of the Crucified One

And those who passed by derided him, wagging their heads and saying, "You who would destroy the temple and rebuild it in three days, save yourself! If you are the Son of God, come down from the cross." So also the chief priests, with the scribes and elders, mocked him, saying, "He saved others; he cannot save himself. He is the King of Israel; let him come down now from the cross, and we will believe in him. He trusts in God; let God deliver him now, if he desires him. For he said, 'I am the Son of God.'"

Matthew 27:40–43

IF THE ENEMIES OF JESUS had any natural human feeling, they would have been silent under the cross where he hung bleeding and dying. Sympathy would have made the watchers serious and thoughtful. When someone is dying, tears are usually shed. At a cruel execution even hardened bystanders are often shaken into silence. But the Lord was denied a quiet hour of death.

The high priests were so full of bitterness that they had the impudence to strut about below the cross, slandering the holy victim of their hatred with malicious jokes and loud mockery. They now make up for the fear this great man caused them by saying he would come on the clouds of heaven. They triumph over him, who only a short time previously was so highly praised, and avenge themselves on him while he is dying. They jeer at his claim to royalty and to being the Son of God. They mock at his power to do miracles. The executioners are amused, and even one of the thieves crucified with Jesus joins in the abuse.

Many who had followed Jesus were admirers only of his outward success. Now that power and fame had left him, they also turned away. They regarded his silence as a confession of guilt. They now looked upon him as a condemned impostor. Angry at having been misled for so long, they too called out jeeringly, "If you are the Son of God, come down from the cross and save yourself!" They also wanted to curry favor with the rulers who were now triumphant.

Of the mass of the people, however, it is written, "The people stood by, watching" (Luke 23:35). That was a gruesome spectacle. Dull-witted and without thought, they gaped at the unprecedented outrage that was taking place. Their great Benefactor, their Messiah, had opened up for them the way of salvation. He had blessed their children, fed the hungry among them, and healed their sick – yet they watched while he was murdered and mocked even while dying. They treated his sacrificial death as something to gratify their curiosity. Not a hand was lifted for him, nor a voice raised! To what depth had the people sunk! To what depth must any nation sink that finds pleasure in bloody spectacles and is fed on public executions.

We also watch – but with a different purpose. We look into the depth of Jesus' heart and admire his behavior and the nobleness and love of which he gives proof in all humiliation. His pure and gentle soul felt more keenly than we can comprehend the outrage done to him by the mockery of his enemies. Moreover, he knew that as the Son of God he could immediately come down from the cross and with a single word destroy his enemies. But he also knew that the scriptures had to be fulfilled that he must become the most despised of men and suffer everything that had been foretold in the

Psalm (Ps. 22:7–19). He was willing to endure what we deserve, to atone for our arrogance, and to save the lost. So he suffered complete wretchedness in silent humility and majesty and even prayed compassionately for those who were slandering him. As for us, we fall on our knees in gratitude and confess, "Jesus, I love you!"

Sixth Week of Lent

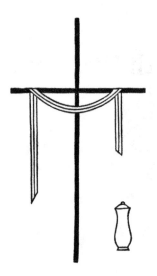

The Criminal's Repentance and His Faith

One of the criminals who were hanged railed at him, saying, "Are you not the Christ? Save yourself and us!" But the other rebuked him, saying, "Do you not fear God, since you are under the same sentence of condemnation? And we indeed justly; for we are receiving the due reward of our deeds; but this man has done nothing wrong." And he said, "Jesus, remember me when you come in your kingdom."

Luke 23:39–42

THE TWO THIEVES appear to be representatives of two opposing directions. One of them founders on the cross; the other is raised up by it. The story of the repentant thief does not teach that every scoundrel can finally slip into the kingdom of heaven through a back door, but it does contain the comfort that even at death conversion is still possible. Nevertheless, this

269

conversion is so unique as to be an exception, and it warns us not to postpone turning to God. Some people deceive themselves terribly by imagining that they will be able to atone for a lifetime's guilt by taking communion on their deathbed.

In the dying hours of this thief everything is great and significant. The nearness of the crucified Savior and the effect of the Holy Spirit on the criminal's soul in its death-struggle is so powerful that a sudden and complete conversion breaks through and this man becomes for all time an example of true repentance and victorious faith.

The fear of God is the beginning and basis not only of wisdom (Ps. 111:10) but also of repentance. The thief's rebuke to his slandering fellow criminal, "Do you not fear God, since you are under the same condemnation?" shows not only moral feeling and manly courage but above all the power of the fear of God that seized him during the crucifixion. The core of repentance is his unsparing judgment of himself: "We indeed are justly condemned, for we are receiving the due reward of our deeds." He excuses nothing. He is completely filled with the consciousness of his guilt, and in the agonies of execution he admits before God and men that the penalty is deserved and just. Then follows his wonderful testimony to the innocence of the Great One who is crucified with him: "But this man has done nothing wrong." The disciples are silent, but to comfort the suffering Lord, stones begin to cry out and to testify to him.

Finally, true repentance must include faith in God's compassion. See how such faith filled the criminal's night with the light of heaven! After relieving his shattered heart by frank and courageous confession, he says pleadingly, "Lord, remember me when you come in your kingdom." A wonderful saying! In the man who is bleeding to death beside him he recognizes a mighty King who has a kingdom, who will not perish in death, but will return some day in victorious majesty. How did the poor criminal receive such sublime insight? He was probably a Jew and familiar with Israel's messianic hope. He would have heard a lot about Christ's deeds and his teaching. That very day, perhaps, carrying his cross behind Jesus, he had heard the Lord's last call to repentance, and he had read the inscription, "King of the Jews," on his cross. On hearing the Lord pray for his enemies, his heart, which yearned for forgiveness, melted within him. He realized Christ's majesty, and in his suffering, faith arose within him: "This man and no other is the Messiah-King who can and will help you."

So his words "Remember me!" contain the request, "When you come again in glory, will you graciously think of the one who is now so close to you in death?"

The conversion, faith, and proclamation to the world contained in these words of the crucified criminal put the apostles and Christians of all times to shame. They served to refresh the Lord in his dying pain. May they serve us as an example on our pathway through life.

80

Sunday Evening

Today You Will Be with Me in Paradise

And Jesus said to him, "Truly, I say to you, today you will be with me in Paradise."

Luke 23:43

IN GETHSEMANE an angel strengthened the Lord, but at Golgotha where no angel was permitted to serve him, the dying criminal was his comfort. The redeemer of the world recognized in him the first of millions who would be saved through his sacrificial death. In him he experienced the first achievement of his great work. Thus the criminal's conversion was to Jesus a refreshing, heavenly drink that filled his breast with redeeming joy. On hearing the heartfelt plea to be remembered, he turns his head to the imploring thief and says the majestic words, "Truly, I say to you, today you will be with me in Paradise!" Those are indeed the words of a king. A kingly heart still beat in his breast. A royal crown was on his head. The pierced hands held his royal scepter and at a glance from his eyes the gates of paradise were opened.

Paradise had been lost to the inhabitants of earth since the first sin, but man could never forget that his cradle had been there: a painful longing always pulled his spirit back to that garden of joy and bliss. What a relief it is that here at Golgotha, where the head of the old serpent is crushed, paradise reappears and the tree of life blossoms anew! With his great promise, the holy sufferer looks beyond the pain of his approaching death into the paradise of his God. Comfort fills his soul: even today he will be in the longed-for place of peace. How wonderful it will be after the struggle and pain of death!

Having come from the bosom of the Father, he knows paradise well, for it was taken from the earth and now adorns the kingdom of heaven. From us, however, it is still hidden as a holy mystery. Yet this much we know from the words of Revelation: paradise is not lost to us. It is still there for us too in heavenly beauty. It is the place of sweet peace where pilgrims find their home and fighters their crown. It is the place where all tears are dried. There the children of God see their Father's face and are united with Christ and one another in the fellowship of holy love.

This paradise is what the Lord now promises the repentant criminal, giving him far more than he asks and understands. When he made his petition he looked into the distant future – and the Lord instead opens up for him the comforting "today." Today, within a few hours, the tortured criminal was to be set completely free from all his wretchedness. He had requested only, "Remember me," wanting to be assured that the king would graciously bear him in mind and help him. Instead of that, in the promise "with me," he is given full community of life with him, the highest honor and most blissful happiness. When he made his request, he had been thinking of an unknown, future kingdom, but Christ immediately opened God's heavenly garden for him. All his sins were to be forgiven him and all punishment canceled. He was never to be separated from the Messiah with whom he was so closely associated in death, but would enter with him the kingdom of blessedness and stay there with him forever. And all that was to take place today! How graciously is this criminal pardoned! Now he can endure all the agonies of his death, for soon, soon they will be over. Soon everything will be good and glorious.

The Lord wants to lead and pardon us too if only we allow ourselves to be roused to repentance and faith by the quiet power of his death. Then he receives us, here and now, into the fellowship of his grace. Already here, he makes us citizens of his kingdom of peace. He shows us that all the suffering on earth is but a short "today" and in the hour of death bears our redeemed souls to his heavenly paradise.

81

Monday Morning

Christ's Farewell to His Own

But standing by the cross of Jesus were his mother and his mother's sister, Mary the wife of Clopas, and Mary Magdalene. When Jesus saw his mother and the disciple whom he loved standing nearby, he said to his mother, "Woman, behold, your son!" Then he said to the disciple, "Behold, your mother!"

John 19:25–27

THE FIRST UTTERANCE from the cross was Christ's prayer for his enemies, the second his merciful reply to the criminal, and the third his words of farewell to his own. In addition to the throngs of enemies and spectators that had gathered at the Place of a Skull, there was a small group of Jesus' closest friends standing close to the cross of the one they loved. It was composed of four persons, three of whom were women. Other faithful women watched from a distance.

Here once more in the story of the Lord's suffering, the dedicated love and deep faithfulness of women shows up in a clear and wonderful light. Heedless of the danger, they had accompanied him all the way to Golgotha. They were the last to remain at the cross and the first at the open tomb. Of the three Marys standing beside the dying Master, his mother deserves special attention. Now that she has to see her son, her Messiah, rejected and bleeding to death on the accursed tree, the hour that was prophesied by Simeon has come: a sword pierces her soul (Luke 2:35). She does not faint, as many a painter has depicted, but strengthened by the unbroken sovereignty of her Son, she endures it consciously and in quiet submission, in keeping with her character, and tries to meet his eyes with her own tearful ones.

One at least of the eleven disciples stands beside the mother. It is John, who saw the Master's glory on Mount Tabor and his inner struggle in Gethsemane and lay close to his breast at the Passover meal. He was the closest of all the disciples to the Lord and the most like him. He had quietly followed the Lord after his capture, had waited humbly in the high priest's courtyard, and then accompanied the Master to Pilate. There he experienced all that took place. He was the closest to the cross at Golgotha. He probably stood – not sobbing with his face covered, but erect, raptly looking at the Crucified One, feeling everything with him, taking it deeply into his soul until all was accomplished.

The Lord with his third utterance from the cross takes leave of these very beloved souls by giving his mother to his friend and his friend to his mother. He had always been poor, but he was poorest of all on the cross. His loved ones were the last treasure of his heart. But from them too he now has to part. He has to experience death. For our sakes he suffers what it means to tear himself away from his nearest and dearest. Completely poor, quite alone, and utterly forsaken, he has to go down into the dark valley of the shadow of death in order to become the Savior of all who are dying. He pays with this deep pain for all the wrong we have done to our parents, brothers, sisters, and friends. When this guilt weighs on our conscience – when our hearts break because we can no longer make up to those who have passed – then forgiveness and comfort can be found in him alone. Only in the one who died of his own free will for our sakes, tearing himself away from the loving arms of his mother and friends, can we find peace.

82

Monday Evening

His Testament of Love

When Jesus saw his mother and the disciple whom he loved standing nearby, he said to his mother, "Woman, behold, your son!" Then he said to the disciple, "Behold, your mother!" And from that hour the disciple took her to his own home.

John 19:26–27

SUFFERING AND DYING on the cross for the immense task of world redemption, the Lord nevertheless represses his own pain and puts himself in the place of his sorrowing mother and friend. Their eyes meet. Their hearts merge, and with a nod of his head the Lord says to his mother, "Woman, behold, your son!" and to his disciple, "Behold, your mother!"

What love, what wisdom there is in this testament! He gives his mother a son, a son like no other. He was not only to care for her but to become her true friend. In years of life together they would go deeper and deeper into the mystery of the person and the work of Christ. For the disciple, no greater sign of trust could be given than to be appointed son to this mother. From that hour he took her to his home and cared for her until she was taken home. What blessing came to this bond of love through their shared memories and insights, and what blessing through the unseen but deeply sensed presence of the great third one.

This testament was not limited to Mary and John. On the contrary, its application spread to include all times and all nations. The Lord's last will kindled a fire of love in his church which has continued in many hearts until today. All true Christians have recognized from his last will that through his death they are entrusted to one another. How many widows and orphans are received and how many abandoned children are cared for and nursed in various institutions and in private homes where the words are borne in mind, "What you did to the least of these my brethren, you did to me" (Matt. 25:40). This charitable activity, permeating and blessing each century, can be regarded as a continuous fulfillment of his testament from the cross.

But alas, obedience to the will of Christ is still lacking in many Christian homes. Unity, peace, and love are not there. Disagreements, touchiness, and misunderstanding separate husbands and wives, parents and children, brothers and sisters, and estrange them from one another. We don't see each other's needs but only the mistakes and shortcomings. No one is ready to bear the other's burden. We grow cool or even hostile toward each other, thus stifling the joy and blessing of family life.

When will that change? When will things get better? Not until we grasp that the Lord's testament applies in the first instance to our closest relations. It will not change until we find each other below his cross and there become reconciled. It will not change until we see that Christ himself commits our relatives to our care and love, saying, "See, that is your father or mother, husband or wife, son or daughter!" The closer we are to the Crucified One, the closer we are to one another. When we become reconciled, bearing and serving one another in him, Christian family life will be a paradise.

83

Tuesday Morning

Darkness

Now from the sixth hour there was darkness over all the land until the ninth hour.

Matthew 27:45

THE LORD'S SEVEN UTTERANCES from the cross shine like seven heavenly stars in the night of his agony. This lasted for six hours: from nine in the morning until three in the afternoon. How long these six hours of torture were! Only in eternity will their content be made known. The first three things that he said were spoken with short intervals between them, soon after the crucifixion. Then the Lord sank once more into deep silence, giving himself up to the experience of his pain of body and of soul.

In his own soul he had to go through the death agony of the whole of humankind. As he hung on the cross, the heat of the sun became more and more burning and the day more sultry. The frightened question may have arisen in some onlookers, "Will God, the Holy and Almighty, really show no sign today?" And indeed, a sign appeared in heaven and on the earth. The midday hour became night. The sun's light failed (Luke 23:45). Deep darkness sank down and shrouded the hill of Golgotha, Jerusalem, and the whole land in its shadow. Alarmed, the spectators became silent. In some the voice of conscience stirred. Some were gripped by the fear of God and left the dreadful place, beating their breasts.

Here the usually hidden, mysterious relationship between the realm of nature and the realm of the spirit is obvious. When Christ was born, a bright and wondrous light shone in the middle of the night. When he died, nature covered its face with a veil of night at midday. Creation mourns the death of its Lord: the sun covers its splendor that it may not see man's dreadful, bloody deed. The Lord had once testified, "I am the light of the world" (John 8:12). What the sun is for the earth, Christ is for humankind. What a horrible grave the earth would be if there were no sun, and what a valley of dry bones the human race without Christ!

The darkness on Good Friday is a similitude of sin and error, death and condemnation. It is above all a picture of what was taking place in the soul of the dying Redeemer. Now he was made to be sin for us; now he was sunk for us in the night of death and condemnation. The sun of his life lost its light. The Father's face was hidden from the Son, and alone, without help or comfort, he had to go through the dark valley of Godforsakenness.

But the sun remains the sun in spite of all eclipses, and Christ remains the Son of God in spite of the night of the cross. In truth, he is perfected through death and judgment as redeemer of the world. So we must not lose courage if we have to go through a dark valley. All darkness is hard. The night of suffering and loneliness is hard, and still harder is the night of sin and guilt. But Christ lives. He is our Savior, our light. Clouds may sometimes hide his face from us, but they are only clouds which must soon disappear. So when our earthly lights go out, we cry trustingly, "The sun may pass away, but Jesus shines brightly in my heart."

84

Tuesday Evening

His Cry of Lamentation

And at the ninth hour Jesus cried with a loud voice, "Eloi, Eloi, lema sabachthani?" which means, "My God, my God, why have you forsaken me?"

Mark 15:34

TOWARD THE END of the three hours of darkness the Lord broke his silence. Like an echo of the twenty-second Psalm, there rang from his tortured breast a cry of lamentation to the darkened heavens, "My God, my God, why have you forsaken me?" How alien, coming from his lips, are the words, "My God, my God!" He had always called the great God simply "Father." Now his soul was filled with such darkness that he could no longer use that endearing name, yet he did not renounce God as a person. Even though the blissful feeling of loving community with the Father was taken from him, he still held firmly to his God with the bare arms of his faith. Thus in his death agony he overcame the blackest temptation of Satan that tried to separate him from his God.

When such temptations try to pull us down into the abyss, when it seems to us that there is no God and no help, then we must do as the Crucified One did. Even without *feeling* faith we must wrestle like Jacob, crying to the Almighty, "Nevertheless, I am continually with you. . . . My flesh and my heart may fail, but God is the strength of my heart and my portion forever" (Ps. 73:23, 26).

"Why?" the Crucified One asks in his death cry, sending the great question of humankind up to heaven – humankind, encompassed by the night of sin, error, and death and yet always struggling for truth. We will always have to question, as long as we are on this earth. But why did he have to ask it? He had come from the Father and in eternity had been one with him in his plan for redemption. Had it become so dark within him that he no longer knew all that? We can only answer with hearts full of gratitude, "You suffered it for us." That is the solution of the mystery. Holy Lamb of God, you send our "Why?" up to the heart of God. You have taken the guilt upon yourself which had to separate us from the Father's sight. That is why you had to sink into this darkness.

"Why have you forsaken me?" the cry continues from the trembling lips. "You – me?" What is contained in this "you"? The whole fatherly heart of God: his love and faithfulness with his divine testimony, "This is my beloved Son in whom I am well pleased" (Matt. 3:17). We must realize that this "me" is the only begotten Son who never even in thought turned away from the Father and who remained obedient to him unto the end. It is he who has to cry, as he sinks into the utmost anguish of death, seeking help in vain, "Why have you forsaken me?"

To be forsaken by God – who can grasp what that means? It is a bitter thing to be deserted in need by all one's friends. It is still more bitter to be cast off by parents or children. But even the most forsaken person can find comfort and refuge in the arms of the heavenly Father. To be forsaken by God, however, is the pain of hell. We deserve nothing less for all our sins. That is why he, who stood security for us with his blood, had to feel in our stead, in the darkest hour of his death agony, the whole curse of Godforsakenness. And through this he opened the way to the Father to us unworthy sinners and assured us fellowship with him.

He is now the God of the widows and orphans and the secure fortress of all who are afraid, lonely, and persecuted. Even the most abandoned criminal can now find grace and be accepted by him for Christ's sake. All those who have been redeemed can build upon the firm assurance that God will not forsake them even in the deepest distress. They can sing with David, "Even though I walk through the valley of the shadow of death I fear no evil; for you are with me" (Ps. 23:4). With Paul they can triumph over all enemies, for "if God is for us, who can be against us?" (Rom. 8:31).

85

Wednesday Morning

I Thirst

After this, Jesus, knowing that all was now finished, said (to fulfill the Scripture), "I thirst."

John 19:28

IN THE SUNNY ORIENT springs of water are considered one of the greatest benefits and so serve as a picture of the most wonderful blessing. "The Lord is my shepherd, I shall not want; he makes me lie down in green pastures. He leads me beside still waters," sings the psalmist (Ps. 23). John describes the happiness of the blessed like this, "They shall hunger no more, neither thirst any more; the sun shall not strike them, nor any scorching heat, for the Lamb will be their shepherd, and he will guide them to springs of living water, and God will wipe away every tear from their eyes" (Rev. 7:16–17).

But these joys of paradise have been dearly bought. The Lord won them for us by thirsting and dying on the cross. His Godforsaken cry expresses the deepest depth of his suffering of soul; the cry, "I thirst!" shows the utmost limit of his physical endurance. Up to this moment he has suffered all his pain in silence. Now, however, his last strength has been exhausted by the terrible struggle in his soul. His wounds burn in the sultry midday heat, and the prophecy is fulfilled, "My heart is like wax; it is melted within my breast; my strength is dried up like a potsherd, and my tongue sticks to my jaws; you lay me in the dust of death" (Ps. 22:14–15). Now he cries out in his death agony.

He humbles himself so far with this dying sigh that he not only lets the rough soldiers and his mocking enemies glimpse the depth of his misery, but he even asks them for a drop to relieve his thirst. When we sinners are dying, our loved ones do all they can to relieve every pain, to offer comfort and help, and to moisten our dry lips. But he had nothing of all that. He, for whose sake all water sources spring, who gives all rivers their courses, and whom the angels would rejoice to serve, in his death has to sigh, "I thirst!"

Why did he have to suffer like this? He was paying the penalty for all our thirst and craving for this world's possessions and enjoyments. The rich man in the place of torment, suffering in the heat, pled in vain for a drop of water to cool his tongue. He was also thirsty. It was eternal thirst for the paradise that was lost to him. We with our worldly desires deserve this misery, but the dying Savior endured it in our stead in his thirst on the cross.

Today, while there is still time, a person can feel appalled at his own worldliness and insatiable desire. If he really mourns the emptiness it has brought to his burned-out heart, he will find the one and only refreshing drink for his languishing soul in our Savior's, "I thirst!" Then in heartfelt gratitude he says, "You did it for me." You did it for me, that I would not have to suffer eternal thirst. You did it for me, that you would be able to lead me to pasture on the meadows of paradise and to the waters of life.

The Drink of Vinegar

And one of them at once ran and took a sponge, filled it with
sour wine, and put it on a reed and gave it to him to drink.
But the others said, "Wait, let us see whether Elijah will
come to save him."

Matthew 27:48–49

IF WE HAD BEEN PRIVILEGED to give our Savior a
refreshing drink, how we would have rejoiced. At Golgotha, however, all he was given was a sponge dipped
in vinegar pressed to his parched lips by a soldier. Possibly this gift was well intentioned. Perhaps it was really
meant to relieve the dying man's torment. But it was a
drink of vinegar, accompanied by jeering and mockery.

The Lord is still offered a drink of vinegar, spiritually speaking, by countless people today. He suffered
for them too, wanting in his compassion to save them.
These are the nominal Christians who reward the Lord

for his agonizing thirst with indifference and ingratitude – even with unbelief and jeering words. Alas, they do not know what they are doing! How happy they could be if they would only begin to be grateful to their faithful Savior and give him a refreshing drink!

Let us be glad that such a longing can be satisfied, that it is really possible for us to give our Redeemer refreshing joy. We can do this by bringing help, comfort, and support to others who are pining under the cross they carry. For when we give a drink of cold water to quench another's thirst, the Lord counts it as though we had given it to him (Matt. 25:40).

But first we must give ourselves completely to our Savior as a real offering of thanksgiving. For in the Lord's physical thirst we may see a similitude of his love yearning for us. He had come to seek the lost, and as he hung on the cross he longed for the completion of his work of grace. He drank the cup of suffering to the dregs with a holy thirst, for at the bottom of the cup shone the heavenly pearl he longed for: the blessedness of the redeemed. It was a powerful thirst, for with his death he wanted nothing less than to bring about the kingdom of glory. He looks down to you and me too, and thirsts to make us his living, eternal possession.

Here the mystery of our own being is revealed to us: he longs for us because we have been created in his image, and without him we cannot live. An infant depends on his mother for everything, so she cannot forget him. In the same way, the Lord cannot leave us, for without him we would be lost. We languish spiritually as long as we do not have him. Only when his love has overwhelmed us do we understand ourselves and know that our deepest longing is for him through whom we are born again as children of God. When our thirst meets his thirst and we become his own in faith and love, then he becomes the source of life to us. Then these words of his are fulfilled in us, "Whoever comes to me shall not hunger, and whoever believes in me shall never thirst" (John 6:35).

87

Thursday Morning

It Is Finished

When Jesus had received the sour wine, he said, "It is finished!"

John 19:30

"IT IS FINISHED!" This loud cry of the dying Savior of the world is the greatest utterance that ever rang out on earth. For now the true High Priest's atoning suffering is finished.

His life had been filled with the light of holy joy, coming as it did from the peace of his pure conscience and his fellowship of love with the Father. As the Lamb of God, however, he carried throughout his pilgrimage on earth all the misery of the lost world.

His actual atoning suffering began in his sorrow unto death in Gethsemane. His capture followed, then his condemnation, and after the night of horror the cruel flogging. This was followed by carrying his cross and the six terrible hours of his deathstruggle. "Where is there sorrow like my sorrow?" (Lam. 1:12) asked the tortured soul of the Crucified One. Finally, when he sank into the night of Godforsakenness, the cup of suffering was drunk to the dregs. He had been obedient unto death, and had made the atoning sacrifice. Now he could cry, "It is finished," and look into the peace of paradise.

The tremendous fight of the Mighty One of the tribe of Judah had been fought to the finish. It was the fierce battle against all the evil in the world, into which he entered immediately on taking on his task. It was the fight against the weakness of his disciples, against the stubbornness of the people, the hypocrisy and wickedness of his enemies, and indeed against the Prince of Darkness and his whole kingdom. For the Lord came into the world to destroy the works of the devil (1 John 3:8). So the devil called up all his cunning, might, and fury to throw the holy Son of Man into eternal night, and our whole human race with him.

It was a terrific struggle against sin, hell, death, and devil in which the Prince of our Salvation had to prove himself. When he cried, "It is finished," the fight was fought. With his triumphant cry, the matchless hero was announcing to his Father in heaven, to the listening angels, and to all generations of humankind that the serpent's head was crushed and the eternal victory won.

The Son of God's work of redemption, which embraced heaven and earth, was accomplished. Lost sinners are now saved, their bonds and fetters broken and the glorious liberty of the children of God restored to them. For guilt is blotted out, sins are forgiven, and the righteousness of God is won. Death has been robbed of its power. No longer is it a cruel tyrant but a messenger of peace leading the redeemed to the heavenly homeland. Now we can say, "For me to live is Christ, and to die is gain" (Phil. 1:21). Thus from the death pangs of Christ a new humanity is born. It gathers in the peaceful kingdom of grace here below, and one day will be perfected on the transfigured earth under the new heaven in the blessed kingdom of eternity.

88

Thursday Evening

The Torn Curtain

And behold, the curtain of the temple was torn in two, from top to bottom.

Matthew 27:51

WHILE THE ONLY BEGOTTEN SON was suffering and dying on the cross, the Father spoke to his blinded people and to all humanity with wordless but shattering signs. The first was the uncanny darkness which lasted from midday until three o'clock. When the darkness was beginning to lift, a second sign appeared: the curtain of the temple was rent. It was a firmly woven, brightly colored curtain, which separated the most holy place from the sanctuary (Exod. 26:31). The most holy place with its golden mercy seat was meant to testify that Jehovah ruled in the midst of his people (Exod. 25:22). But the curtain hiding God's glory from all eyes was to proclaim to the people that perfect atonement and community with God did not yet exist. There was as yet no way open for sinners to have access to him. That is why the prophet declares, "Your iniquities have made a separation between you and your God, and your sins have hidden his face from you" (Isa. 59:2). Only on the Day of Atonement was the high priest permitted to enter the most holy place after making an offering for his own purification. Then he sprinkled the mercy seat with the blood of a lamb, while the people knelt in the forecourt.

On the day Jesus died, at three o'clock, the hour of solemn prayer, many people would have gathered in the temple vestibules and in the forecourt. The darkness which had settled over both city and country must have depressed and frightened them. The sanctuary of the temple, however, was brightened by the flames of the seven-branched candlestick. The priests were attending to their duties, and worshipping Israelites had gathered about them.

At the moment when at Golgotha the crucified Savior gave his cry of victory, "It is finished," the great curtain was torn in two from top to bottom. To the amazement and horror of all present, the most holy place which had always been concealed lay open to the gaze of all.

This miracle was to make known what was now taking place in the invisible world. By his death the true High Priest, who was at the same time the Lamb of God, had offered the fully valid atoning sacrifice. He had removed the barrier that separated sinners from God's holiness. He himself entered the most holy place of heaven in the glory of his wounds, coming before his Father with the blood of the covenant. Thus the guilt of the whole world was atoned for, the work of redemption for all sinners was accomplished, and the portal of grace was opened to all, giving free access to God.

Now heaven is open for us as well. The heart of eternal compassion has been opened to us. God is our Father; we are his children. Who will separate us from the love of God (Rom. 8:35)? Our prayers rise up to him, and his answers come down to us. Each celebration of the Lord's Supper deepens our fellowship with him. We walk on earth but our home is in heaven. When the time comes for us to die, the last curtain that still hides God's face from us will fall. We will leave all pain behind and, purified by the blood of the Lamb, will enter the Father's holy city to celebrate the Lord's Supper in heaven.

89

Good Friday Morning

Father, into Your Hands I Commit My Spirit

Then Jesus, calling out with a loud voice, said, "Father, into your hands I commit my spirit!"

Luke 23:46

GOOD FRIDAY, the day the world's Redeemer died, has come again. Let the people of God be still! Be still, my soul! Into this stillness, may the farewell cry of the dying Lord resound.

With the words, "It is finished," the decisive battle was won. The full victory of light was achieved, the tremendous work of world redemption was done. The Lamb of God had endured his suffering. It was now quiet at the cross on Golgotha. Now the Lord could depart in peace.

His last words were once more a prayer: "Father, into your hands I commit my spirit." He could call on his Father once more. Ever since his boyhood he had wanted nothing else than his Father's will. His well-being, his peace of soul, lay in his fellowship of love with the Father. He was completely united with him. Even in Gethsemane he had called him "Abba," and his first utterance from the cross was a prayer to the Father. Now that he had at last gone through the valley of Godforsakenness and the darkness had given way, he could also address his last words to the Father. God's face shone upon him again. God's heart was once more open to him and there was no longer a cloud between Father and Son.

"Into your hands I commit my spirit." As the Lord's lament was taken from Psalm 22, his dying word of peace is an echo of Psalm 31. From this we learn what filled the soul of the Crucified One during his death agonies. It was the prophetic strains of the word of God which were now finding fulfillment through his suffering and serving him as a lamp to his feet and a light to his path (Ps. 119:105).

He committed his spirit into the hands of his Father. To the psalmist, these hands depicted the care of God guiding, protecting, and blessing. These almighty hands of love guide not only the stars in their courses and the nations in their historical development, but also the individual children of God on all their paths. Happy are those who trust the guidance of these hands with their whole heart! None knew these hands better than the only begotten Son. He longed with the whole strength of his filial love to be back in the opened arms of the Father. "Father, glorify me with the glory that I had with you before the world existed," he had prayed after the farewell meal (John 17:5). Now he no longer needed to pray as a weak human being. He had accomplished all that was necessary to lay full claim to the glory of the Father. So he said, "Into your hands I commit my spirit."

This giving over of his spirit, however, also contains the serious fact of death: the separation of soul and body. The Lord had to personally go through the experience of death if he was to conquer death for us. His spirit also had to wander outside his body until Easter morning. That is why he now committed it into his Father's hands. He had no need to ask to be forgiven. He was God's own Son. Nothing could separate him from his Father. His longing was now satisfied. Now his tired, tortured spirit returned to the paradise of his God, to the place of blessed peace where the air of heaven would revive him, the angels serve him, and where he would rest in his Father's bosom.

Through his death he has opened the way to heaven for all his redeemed. He has made the valley of the shadow of death bright and has changed the bitterness of death to a peaceful homecoming.

90

Good Friday Evening

The Death of Jesus

And he bowed his head and gave up his spirit.
John 19:30

WITH THESE SHORT AND SIMPLE WORDS the Gospel records the greatest fact in world history: the death of Jesus Christ, Son of God and Son of Man. After he spoke his last words, his actual death took place, the separation of soul and body. His prayer had ascended to heaven; his pallid head bowed down to the earth. The Son of Man had had no cradle in Bethlehem, and he had no bed at Golgotha. Even in death he had no place to lay his head (Matt. 8:20).

The Lord was surely dead, as the stab with the spear showed. He died as we all have to die, but he died of his own free will in perfect obedience to his Father's merciful, eternal plan and in burning love for the lost world. Yet this fact did not free him from the pain of death. He felt the agonizing pain of the soul's tearing away from the body. Indeed, his death was infinitely harder and more painful than that of any other pilgrim on earth. For he had to take upon his conscience the guilt of the whole world, the sins of all sinners. He had to take the punishment of all the condemned into his pure, sensitive heart. At the same time, as regards his own person he was able to come before God's countenance with the peace of a completely clear conscience. He knew the joy and glory into which his spirit was now to enter. If we had such a clear insight into what awaits us in heaven, all fear and dread of death would leave our hearts. With what longing we would then approach the goal of our pilgrimage!

But in addition to this, Christ had his incomparable love to humanity. The purpose of his death was their redemption and happiness. He foresaw with prophetic vision the outcome of his sacrificial death. He saw that it would embrace and renew the whole world. This vision must have lifted him, as on eagle's wings, out of the misery and torture of crucifixion and filled his dying pain with heavenly joy. Thus the tremendous moment when he bowed his head and gave up his spirit will be praised throughout all eternities. It gave birth to a new humankind, it founded the kingdom of God on earth, and it prepared the way for eternal heavenly glory.

Now it is possible for Stephen, while being stoned to death by his enemies, to see heaven open. Paul can say with yearning, "I would rather be away from the body and at home with the Lord" (2 Cor.5:8). All the martyrs can daringly testify, "Death is swallowed up in victory" (1 Cor. 15:54). Comforted and in deep peace, we too can now commit our loved ones who have gone home to the heavenly Father's loving arms, and when the hour strikes for us, we can confess with joy, "For to me to live is Christ, and to die is gain" (Phil. 1:21).

91

Saturday Morning

The Consequences
of Jesus' Death

*And the earth shook, and the rocks were split. The tombs
also were opened. And many bodies of the saints who had
fallen asleep were raised, and coming out of the tombs after
his resurrection they went into the holy city and appeared
to many. When the centurion and those who were with him,
keeping watch over Jesus, saw the earthquake and what
took place, they were filled with awe, and said, "Truly this
was the son of God."*

*And all the crowds that had assembled for this spectacle,
when they saw what had taken place, returned home
beating their breasts.*

*So the soldiers came and broke the legs of the first, and of
the other who had been crucified with him. But when they
came to Jesus and saw that he was already dead, they did*

*not break his legs. But one of the soldiers pierced his side
with a spear, and at once there came out blood and water.*

Matthew 27:51–54; Luke 23:48; John 19:32–34

THE EVENTS that took place in nature and in human
life at the time of Jesus' death correspond to its great
significance. As the dying Savior bows his head in
death, the earth quakes and the rocks split: nature rings
the death knell for her Lord. In this we can recognize
a prototype of the terrors of the judgment in which the
old earth will one day sink in ruins. At the same time
we can see a heralding of the new earth upon which
the yearning of the whole creation is to be gloriously
stilled. But human hearts that are not shattered by the
death of Christ are harder than the rocks of Jerusalem.

Many tombs were opened by the earthquake.
Many believers of former times arose and appeared
to living people in the royal city who were of the same
mind with them. The death of Christ brought about a
decisive change in the visible and the invisible world.
God-fearing men of the old covenant who had once
waited for him in faith and hope are now to be with
him and enter the heavenly paradise. The prison of the
grave is opened and the glorious liberty of the children

of God proclaimed. The Lord's words, "All who are in the tombs will hear the voice of the Son of God," begin to find fulfillment (John 5:28). A prophetic breath of the great spring of resurrection passes through the Holy Land, proclaiming that Christ's death is our life. Today's Christendom must consider that it is high time to awake from sin's sleep of death.

The Gospel does not say what Caiaphas and his band felt about the darkness, the rending of the curtain, and the earthquake. However, from the demand they made soon afterwards that the holy tomb be sealed, we can see that they did not enjoy their hoped-for Sabbath rest. A secret horror, an embarrassing fear of the great Crucified One, filled their souls, and the worm that does not die (Mark 9:48) began to gnaw at their hearts.

But the common people who were still standing at Golgotha beat their breasts and went home. If that meant a real repentance filled with fear, then their feeling of agitation may be looked upon as a forerunner of the Day of Pentecost with its great harvest.

One beautiful consequence of Christ's death, however, was the confession of the pagan centurion below the cross. He had not taken his eyes off Jesus. He had been moved by his seven utterances and was shaken to the depth of his being when the earth quaked.

Finally, invoking God, he acknowledged the great Crucified One. He testified before heaven and earth that this man who had been crucified as an evildoer was not only just and innocent (as Pilate had already stated) but the Son of God. Blessed centurion, to have come to Jesus, believing and praising God, as the first fruits of the pagan peoples.

It is a miracle that in the midst of his enemies and executioners the dying Savior could gather and build up his church! The water and the blood that flowed when the lance pierced his holy body indicate the same thing. They are a mysterious allusion to the two sacraments by means of which the Lord extends his church, gives her new life, and makes her holy. Children are born to him out of the water of baptism as dew is born of the dawn. He feeds the weary and heavy-laden in the Holy Supper with his precious blood and consecrates them to be conquerors of death. Thus the wonders that took place at Jesus' death harmonize in the eternal song of praise, "Worthy is the Lamb who was slain, to receive wisdom and might and honor and glory and blessing!" (Rev. 5:12).

92

Saturday Evening

His Burial

And when evening had come, since it was the day of Preparation, that is, the day before the Sabbath, Joseph of Arimathea, a respected member of the council, who was also himself looking for the kingdom of God, took courage and went to Pilate and asked for the body of Jesus. Pilate was surprised to hear that he should have already died. And summoning the centurion, he asked him whether he was already dead. And when he learned from the centurion that he was dead, he granted the corpse to Joseph.

Nicodemus also, who earlier had come to Jesus by night, came bringing a mixture of myrrh and aloes, about seventy-five pounds in weight. So they took the body of Jesus and bound it in linen cloths with the spices, as is the burial custom of the Jews. Now in the place where he was crucified there was a garden, and in the garden a new tomb in which no one had yet been laid. So because of the Jewish day of Preparation, since the tomb was close at hand, they laid Jesus there.

The women who had come with him from Galilee followed and saw the tomb and how his body was laid. Then they returned and prepared spices and ointments. On the Sabbath they rested according to the commandment.

Mark 15:42–45; John 19:39–42; Luke 23:55–56

THE WORK OF RECONCILIATION was accomplished. The Son had given his spirit into his Father's hands. But his pale body still hung on the cross in the light of the evening sky. Golgotha was now quiet and deserted. Only the women from Galilee and probably also John stood mourning at the cross. Love still burned in their hearts, but all their hope had died with the Master. They were waiting for Nicodemus and Joseph, two members of the council who wanted to see to the burial. These two had not consented to the enemy's plan, but had hitherto only followed Jesus in secret. In the glowing fire of the Master's suffering and death, however, the dross had been smelted from their faith, and the refined gold had come to light. The secret admirers had suddenly become courageous believers.

Joseph had begged Pilate for the body of Jesus. Now he came bringing fine linen. Nicodemus came too with a supply of myrrh and aloes. When he looked up at the dead face, he might have remembered the mysterious words of the Lord: "As Moses lifted up the serpent in the wilderness, so must the Son of Man be lifted up" (John 2:14).

With gentle care the precious body was taken from the cross, washed clean, and swathed in linen filled with spices. Then the mourners bore him quietly to the new rock-hewn grave in Joseph's nearby garden. Here he was laid on a couch of myrrh and aloes, and the opening of the tomb was closed with a great stone. Jesus, who in life had not a place to lay his head, was buried like a rich man as had been foretold. And he who had died for the guilt of others was laid in the grave of another man.

While his disciples were sunk in hopelessness, his enemies remembered with dread that he had repeatedly said that he would rise again on the third day. In their fear, they saw to it that the holy tomb was sealed and a watch set. Meanwhile the faithful women sat in Joseph's garden until the sun went down, watching with tear-filled eyes the tomb where their treasure lay.

Aware that our life too is hid with Christ in God, let us join these women in spirit. Let us contemplate our Savior's grave. All the sin and guilt of our lives is buried forever. The earth has been hallowed by the Sabbath rest of the Lord in Joseph's garden, the earth in which his own are henceforth laid to rest. Our graves have become holy sleeping places where God's children rest in peace after labor and striving, suffering and tears. We take Jesus right into our hearts, and when we go to sleep we await a joyful awakening in the bright morning of eternity.

Thus in the light of Christ's grave our graves have become transfigured to places of the most wonderful hope. The grave could not hold the Prince of Life. On the third day Christ broke through the rock and seal and rose as victor over sin, death, and the devil. Our hope too is in the resurrection.

Related titles from Plough

Watch for the Light
Readings for Advent and Christmas

Dietrich Bonhoeffer, Annie Dillard, Thomas Merton, Kathleen Norris, C. S. Lewis, Henri Nouwen, and others

These fifty devotions invite the reader to contemplate the great themes of Christmas and the significance that the coming of Jesus has for each of us – not only during Advent, but every day. Whether dipped into at leisure or used on a daily basis, *Watch for the Light* gives the phrase "holiday preparations" new depth and meaning.

Bread and Wine
Readings for Lent and Easter

Wendell Berry, G. K. Chesterton, Blaise Pascal, Dorothy Sayers, John Updike, Oscar Wilde, and others

A time for self-denial, soul-searching, and spiritual preparation, Lent is traditionally observed by daily reading and reflection. This collection will satisfy the growing hunger for meaningful and accessible devotions. Culled from the wealth of twenty centuries, the selections in *Bread and Wine* are ecumenical in scope, and represent the best classic and contemporary Christian writers.

available at **www.plough.com**
PO box 398, Walden, NY 12586, USA
Brightling Rd, Robertsbridge, East Sussex TN32 5DR, UK
4188 Gwydir Highway, Elsmore, NSW 2360, Australia

CPSIA information can be obtained
at www.ICGtesting.com
Printed in the USA
JSHW060037040123
35676JS00002B/3